MW00622752

Mad Dogs, Marbles, and Rock Fights

a memoir

Scott Eubanks

Scott Eubanks

Copyrighted Material

Mad Dogs, Marbles, and Rock Fights: A Memoir
Copyright © 2017 by Scott Eubanks. All Rights Reserved.
No part of this publication may be reproduced, stored in a retrieval system or transmitted, in any form or by any means—electronic, mechanical, photocopying, recording or otherwise—without prior written permission from the publisher, except for the inclusion of brief quotations in a review.

For information about this title or to order other books and/or electronic media, contact the publisher:
Scott Eubanks
www.EastTexasHappy.com
hello@easttexashappy.com

Elementary school photo of author on front cover.

ISBN: 978-0-9986641-6-3 (print)
          978-0-9986641-7-0 (eBook)

Printed in the United States of America
Cover and Interior design: 1106 Design

Dedicated to the memory of three special women who relentlessly urged me to lift the lid off my imagination and free my creativity. They were my aunts Bonnie Jewel Eubanks Kash and Phyllis Faye Eubanks Berry, along with my unique high school English teacher, Miss Selma Brötze.

Lastly, Mad Dogs, Marbles, and Rock Fights: A Memoir, *is dedicated to my beloved mother, Zelma Chance Eubanks, who spent her lifetime thinking I could do anything I wanted to do if I set my mind to it.*

Contents

Author's Note

*M*ad *Dogs, Marbles, and Rock Fights: A Memoir* is not an autobiography. It is a recollection of a time—the 1950s and early 1960s—a place—Marshall, Texas—and the characters of that time and place from the perspective of a young boy who did his early growing up then, there, and with those characters. It is a non-fiction work, although I am sure those with whom I spent my early years in Marshall will point out my misremembrances. I once read that we are great at revisionist remembering. Well, maybe a little.

When you read this memoir, you will discover I loved living there and then. I also loved the characters with whom I shared those times. There were rough patches in my early years, of course, but my good memories blissfully overpower the bad ones and keep them shut away in the recesses of my brain. Selective dementia has its advantages.

Perhaps I shall someday write a book about the dark cloud that hung over much of America, and certainly Marshall, in the 1950s. That cloud was segregation and the guilt that came with it. With the birth of the Civil Rights Movement, angst, fear, uncertainty, and sometimes conflict could be smelled on the breath of Marshall. As our nation struggled to right the wrong of injustice, so did Marshall. While I in no way want to minimize the hardships many Marshallites and other Americans suffered in their battles for justice and equality, those discussions belong in another book. This book celebrates the joys of life from the eyes of a small boy and his friends—a boy who didn't have to shoulder the weight of the world until adulthood. If I have written this book the way I intended, it will reflect the happiness I enjoyed as a child, and it will put a smile on your face that will last quite some time.

Mad Dogs, Marbles, and Rock Fights: A Memoir covers my life from about age four through the sixth grade. It's a short period of time, but even back then I knew I wanted to commit it to memory. I was "living the good life," and I purposely took the time to embed it all in my memory. Even today, I remember where most all my classmates sat in each classroom. I remember the clothes they wore, the sounds of their laughter, their middle names, and, in many cases, their birthdays. I tapped into all those rich memories to compose this memoir. You will get to know the characters, and I'll bet you fall in love with them like I did so many years ago.

Mad Dogs, Marbles, and Rock Fights: A Memoir has no plot line running through it. The chapters are not in sequential order. It speaks of no great tragedies that had to be overcome. It doesn't preach a certain moral code, and I guess, in all honesty, it's not particularly cerebral. It's light, it's simple, it's clean, it's uplifting, and it's funny. It is also historical, because it implies and records a simpler age in America, and, perhaps, an almost naive purity that existed during that time. This story is not about me. It's about a whole slew of kids who grew up together. My life alone doesn't merit a biography, but *our* story is worth telling.

Hop on the bicycle of your imagination and ride the streets of Marshall in the 1950s and 1960s with the kids and characters of Southside. You'll have a blast.

Chapter 1
Marshall, Texas – My Hometown

I cannot write a meaningful memoir of having grown up in Marshall, Texas in the 1950s and '60s without putting a face on Marshall and giving it a personality. Those are tough assignments, but I will try.

Marshall was founded in 1842, and named for U.S. Supreme Court Chief Justice John Marshall. It is in the Piney Woods of Northeast Texas, only about eighteen miles from the Louisiana line. Because of its location butting up to Louisiana and Arkansas and its rich soil, East Texas was considered part of "Little Dixie." The same could be said of Marshall. Cotton was king in Marshall, just as it was in the 19th-century South; and it remained that way until the Civil War ended and Jay Gould ran his Texas & Pacific Railroad through the heart of

Marshall in 1868. It's interesting to note that Marshall was the fourth-largest city in Texas by 1860.

It's impossible to separate Marshall from the Confederacy. While much—if not most—of Texas was somewhat indifferent about slavery and the War, Marshall's and East Texas's devotion to a cotton economy spurred its citizens to help convince Texas to join the Confederacy. It probably wasn't too tough of a sale because Texans generally would have resented the federal government imposing its will on the state no matter what the issue was. Texas still doesn't cotton to federal infringement on its self-rule.

In a historical oddity, Marshall served as the Confederate capital of Missouri 1863–1865. In fact, Marshall became the headquarters for Confederate operations west of the Mississippi River in 1863. Additionally, Marshall had a factory employing more than forty people who made Confederate hats, blankets and saddle blankets. It also had a factory on the outskirts of town making gunpowder for the Confederacy.

The following inscription etched on a statue honoring the Confederate soldier that stands at Marshall's courthouse leaves little doubt as to where the city's loyalties were placed during the Civil War:

> Soldier, you in the wreck of gray,
> With the brazen belt of the C.S.A.,
> Take our love and our tears today:

Take them, all that we have to give,
And by God's help while our hearts shall live,
It shall keep in its faithful way
The campfires lit for the men in gray—
Aye, 'til trumpet sounds far away
And the silver bugles of heaven play.
And the roll is called at Judgement Day!

When the South lost the Civil War, Marshall slipped away from its economic reliance on cotton. Because of the arrival of Gould's railroad, Marshall rather quickly established itself as a commerce center and a stopping-off place for thousands of those heading westward for a new life. The Texas & Pacific Railroad established its repair and manufacturing shops in Marshall and built its local employment to well into the thousands by the 1950s. It even built the T&P Hospital in Marshall for its employees. It was a railroad town, and it prospered as such until the shops left Marshall for Dallas in the 1970s. Today, Marshall's population is down from more than 26,000 to about 22,000, about 60 percent of which is African American, a percentage that hasn't changed much since I was a small boy. It is a tired town, and it wears its economic woes on the faces of its buildings and its people. While most all vestiges of its Little Dixie past have faded with time, the conversational accent still lingers. Those listening to East Texans talk often think they are hearing someone from Georgia or Alabama.

When people ask me where I'm from, I proudly tell them, "Marshall, Texas." Folks unfamiliar with Texas usually assume all of Texas looks like the Texas they've seen in John Wayne Westerns—open, barren and dusty. It surprises them when I tell them Marshall and East Texas look more like the South and East of our country rather than scenes from *Lonesome Dove* or *The Last Picture Show*. Marshall is green with rolling hills, tall trees and lots of rivers, streams, ponds and lakes in and around it. Marshall gets fifteen inches more rain per year than Seattle does. It is brimming with antebellum and Victorian houses, historic oaks and cemeteries with the graves of founders of Texas, war heroes and powerful political leaders.

As a boy running around town, I remember many of the old homes still had iron tethering rings set in the concrete in front of the houses. Some were posts with the rings on their tops, often dangling from an iron horse's nose, and some were simple rings sunk directly into the old sidewalks. It was easy to imagine horses and carriages tied up to these rings in my hometown's glorious past. I think antique-hungry scavengers have probably cleaned Marshall out of those charming symbols of a bygone era by now. It takes very little imagination to stand in Marshall's old downtown and envision the ghosts of the powerful, the pampered, the strong, the creative, the brave and the optimistic folks that made it a Texas nerve center in its heyday. I think that heyday lasted through the 1950s, but historians may disagree.

Whenever I revisit Marshall, I can still hear the sounds and smell the aromas that were prevalent when I stood on those same spots as a boy. At the intersection of Grand and South Washington, the smell of popcorn from the Paramount and Lynn theaters still bathes the area, even though both "picture shows" are long gone. If I walk a block south or west, the smell of fresh baked bread and cream-filled treats fill my head, even though Melancon's Bakery is long gone. If I move two blocks to the east, the smell of hot steam laced with starch from City Laundry and the magical aromas emanating from the Tiny Grill's hamburger grill flood my senses, even though City Laundry and the Tiny Grill are long gone, too. When I cross to the north side of Grand Avenue, which is U.S. 80, I still hear the coupling of colossal railcars down at the shops. The brutish sound of heavy metal slamming into other heavy metal not only echoed through the neighborhoods, it seemed as though it was shaking the earth. It sounded and felt very powerful, and I guess it should have, as the railyards and shops were the economic locomotives that powered Marshall's midcentury economy. Shift changes at the shops and nearby foundry were signaled by the crystal-clear sound of the steam whistle that could be heard throughout most of Marshall. But, like too much of the Marshall of my childhood, the shops, foundry and the T&P Hospital have vanished. The whistle is now silent.

5

Downtown Marshall was (and still is) filled with one, two and three story buildings that radiated in all directions from the courthouse square. Most were built from the 1860s through the 1940s. The older they were, the more ornate and interesting they were. Some parts of downtown looked as though they belonged in the central cities described in a Charles Dickens novel, while other parts seemed to fall from the pages of an Edna Ferber book. I loved downtown Marshall and its neat, old buildings. In my mind's eye, I can still see them, even though many of them are now gone. When urban renewal swept through America's towns and cities, too many great, old, character-rich buildings were gobbled up by the hungry bulldozers that roamed our streets in search of helpless buildings. We replaced those jewels with vacant lots that are still waiting for the redevelopment that will never come.

The main parking areas in downtown were on the east and west sides of the old courthouse. It was a bit strange how most of the shoppers parked on the east side, while the west side was unofficially reserved for cattlemen and farmers and their pickup trucks and livestock trailers. Those parking on the east side parked and went about their business. The westsiders, on the other hand, sat around on lowered tailgates talking about whatever farmers and cattlemen talk about. There was always an audible hum emanating from those fellows, punctuated by exclamations, laughter, country cussin', the pawing of their boots and the occasional splat of tobacco juice hitting the bricks.

Livestock trades took place and there was always a cattleman or two who brought a cow to sell to Solomon's Grocery Store, which was located one block north of the square, next door to the library. If Mr. Solomon was buying, the seller would park on the street in front of the grocery store and unload his cow. Mr. Solomon would usually walk the cow across the library lawn to the back of his store and shoot it in the head with a .22 rifle. While still in the alley, he would quarter the dead cow with a saw, gut it, and then drag it into the back of the store for butchering. The head, hooves, guts and other inedible parts of Old Bossy would be thrown into fifty-five-gallon drums, which were later hauled off to wherever they dumped such things or given to pig farmers who would feed it all to their pigs. For some reason, Mr. Solomon occasionally performed this shoot, saw-up, clean-up and drag job in front of his store, on one of Marshall's major downtown streets. As a boy, I watched this scene play out numerous times. It didn't frighten me or scar me for life. It was just the way things were done back then. It was normal, not traumatic. Today, when I stand in front of what used to be Solomon's, I can vividly recall the sound of the rifle and smell the fresh blood of the cow. If Solomon's was still there, I would go in and inhale the smell of fresh meat and of produce as I had so many times in my youth, but, of course, Solomon's is long gone.

We had Coca-Cola and Dr. Pepper bottling plants in downtown Marshall. Mr. Mann's Dr. Pepper plant was located

7

next to our main fire station. One could stand on the sidewalk in front of it and stare through a large plate glass window as an endless row of bottles passed by on a conveyor belt on their way to the filling and capping machines. Oh, Lord, those Dr. Peppers looked good to a penniless boy on a hot summer day. I usually stopped by there for a lustful look each Saturday morning on my way home from the Kiddie Show (see the next chapter). I would also stick my head in the fire station and say hello to Misters Warnstaff, Hensley and Kuykendahl, long-serving firemen who would let me go upstairs to play pool if they weren't busy and if the chief was away.

Marshall was prosperous and alive in the '50s and '60s. It had three colleges, two hospitals, scholastically and athletically strong high schools and pretty girls. Two of the colleges were Bishop College and Wiley College which, at the time, were two of the eight largest Negro colleges in the world. We also had East Texas Baptist College (now a university), which turned out scores of preachers year after year. Bishop moved to Dallas in the early '60s, but Wiley and ETBU are still going strong. Marshall is down to one hospital now, but it's a big regional medical center. Marshall still has bright students, good athletes, and as for the pretty girls, well, they are still pretty, just as their mothers and grandmothers were.

For a relatively small place, Marshall has an impressive list of famous alumni, including Lady Bird Johnson,

Bill Moyers (then known as "Billy Don"), the boxer George Foreman, NFL Hall of Fame quarterback Y. A. Tittle and Susan Howard, who costarred on *Dallas* (real name Jeri Lynn Mooney). Additionally, Tex Ritter and the "Country Gentleman" Jim Reeves grew up a few miles down U.S. 59 in Carthage, Texas. I've always been proud of our hometown folks that "done good."

Downtown was fun for a kid. It was a happy place, filled with people to see, things to see, and much to wish for. All of the merchants knew your parents, and they knew you. They tussled your hair when you visited them, and they took the time to make you feel important. Folks always nodded and spoke to those they met on the sidewalks. People made a point to be friendly—a neat thing to do. Today, it seems as though when you speak to strangers you pass on the sidewalk, they may very well look at you like you are nuts or glare at you like you invaded their private space. Pity.

Marshall was big enough to hide in, small enough to allow one to know most of its residents, pretty enough to be proud of, and historical enough to be rich in character. Marshall, and particularly its downtown, was a multifaceted playground for those of us growing up there in the 1950s. We had it good, and played with our hometown like it was a close friend.

I don't know if I've given Marshall a face and a personality for you, but I hope so. Remembering my hometown has caused me to love it again the way I did when I was growing up. Marshall is old and a bit tired now. And its wrinkles, droopiness and infirmities are readily visible, just as they are in the old and tired people who grew up there in the 1950s. The passage of time relentlessly nibbles away at everyone's and everything's strength and beauty, and Marshall has not been spared. While I do see Marshall as she is now, I can also see Marshall as she was. She was strong. She was gorgeous. She was as nurturing to me as a loving grandmother is to a needy child. Opie had Mayberry. I had Marshall.

Chapter 2
Nickel Pickles and the Kiddie Show

My friends and I went downtown to the Kiddie Show at the Paramount Theater nearly every Saturday morning. It was a real social gathering, and the first order of business was to decide who you were going to sit with. I usually opted to sit with girls. One week it might be Shirley Munden, the next Suzanne George, and the next Salley Whitener. Kiddie Show romances usually only lasted a week or two. I remember snuggling with Suzanne one Saturday when she was wearing a tasseled leather jacket. I remember it because the lingering smell of the leather was so strong I smelled as though I had been cuddling with a calf.

Once the lights went out, the big screen flickered to life and we were treated with a serial that lasted about ten to fifteen minutes. It might have been a *Dick Tracy*, a *Buck Rogers*, a *Captain America*, a *Commander Cody*, a *Superman*, a *Batman* or a

Zorro. It would usually end as the star fell to what was certain to be his death. It always left you hanging, eager to return the following Saturday to see if the hero bit the dust or lived to fight another battle. The problem was there was no continuity between the serials. One week Superman was dying from an overdose of Kryptonite, and the next week Commander Cody was about to collide with an asteroid.

The serial was followed by about five cartoons—the highlights of our Kiddie Show. We loved Bugs, Tom and Jerry, Goofy, Woody Woodpecker and Yosemite Sam. We hated the cartoons that invited us to sing along by following the bouncing ball as it bounced from word to word of the lyrics as they trailed along the bottom of the screen. They were always sickeningly sweet with characters like Bambi just standing around grinning with butterflies perched on their noses, or an overly cheerful Mickey Mouse singing a love song to Minnie Mouse in his nerve-gnawing high-pitched voice. When the music started, Bambi or Mickey would hop from lyric to lyric to help keep us from getting lost. We booed the musical cartoons. The only four people I ever saw singing along were Becky Fitch, Joy Williams, Kay Hightower and Johnny George. Obviously, they liked music more than most of us.

After the cartoons, we had about a fifteen-minute intermission. During this time, we ate the lunches we brought from home, or if you were a rich kid, you ran across the street to the Waffle Shop and bought a burger to bring back to the theater. We hit the concession stand hard during this intermission to spend however much money we had for a Coke (we called all soft drinks "Cokes"), popcorn, Milk Duds, Sugar Babies or a Butterfinger. Large dill pickles were available for a nickel a piece, and they were very popular. When the pickle price jumped to a dime, kids were as mad as old wet hens for a couple of weeks, but they moved on.

The showing of the feature movie was the grand finale of our Kiddie Show. It was a B movie to be sure. When the movie was a Western, we might see The Lone Ranger, Hopalong Cassidy, Roy Rogers, Gene Autry, Lash LaRue, or The Cisco Kid. Or it might have been a shoot-'em-up starring Randolph Scott, Scott Brady, Richard Egan, or Guy Madison. Options on the sci-fi/monster slate included *The Blob, The Creature from the Black Lagoon, Them!, The Fly, The Thing, Godzilla, The Day the Earth Stood Still, The Body Snatchers* or some outer-space thriller starring John Agar, Richard Denning or Richard Carlson. We saw lots of Tarzan movies and loved them. Johnny Weissmuller was the original Tarzan, but as he aged, retired or was fired, actors like Gordon Scott and Ron Ely took over. Their arrival in the jungle also brought color with it. Cool. Cheetah was a real fan favorite. *Abbott and Costello* was another favorite that was a crowd pleaser, as were movies starring Jerry Lewis and Dean Martin. We preferred laughing to singing.

Not counting my Saturday visits to the Kiddie Show, trips to the Paramount were rare for our family. Mother only went to see Bible-based extravaganzas like *The Robe*, *The Ten Commandments* and *The Bible*. I always got to go with her to these "teaching" movies. My dad either wasn't into movies or felt as though he couldn't afford it, because, to my knowledge, he only went to the movies twice. He went to see *High Noon*, starring Gary Cooper, and *Bad Day at Black Rock*, with Spencer Tracy. My brothers Homer and Robert went to the movies a lot, usually with dates. However, one night they decided to let me tag along with them as they went to see *The House of Wax*, a 3-D thriller starring Vincent Price. Three-D was new at that time and the audience jumped, dodged, screamed and ducked every time Price swung into our laps. I must have been too young for such a spooky, scary adventure, because, according to my brothers, I screamed constantly and tried repeatedly to flee the theatre. In short, I totally embarrassed both brothers. I was off their invitation list from then on.

It wouldn't be a complete story about the Kiddie Show or the Paramount without some mention of the owner/ manager of the Paramount, Mr. Gelling. He ruled the theater with an iron fist, and we thought of him as merciless when it came to doling out punishment for our rowdy behavior. He stood very erect and always wore a white shirt, tie and dark suit, with the coat buttoned. Honestly, he looked more like a funeral director or a prison warden than a guy who ran a theater. He oozed formality and sternness as he strolled the aisles with flashlight in hand searching for Coke-cup poppers, popcorn-bag poppers, and anyone else annoying the other movie-goers. When he sensed or witnessed an infraction of manners, he spotlighted the offender with his flashlight, removed him from his seat, and took him to his office. At best, the felon got a firm talking-to along with a threat of expulsion for a second offense. At worst, the guilty was escorted out of the Paramount and dumped onto the sidewalk. If the trouble maker had really fouled up, he was banned for some period of time Mr. Gelling thought fit the crime. Those banned boys who dared try to ignore the ban and sneak in were inevitably caught by Mr. Gelling, who re-kicked them out and extended their ban. I referred to the guilty parties as males, but, in truth, I remember Frankie Lawson and Charlotte Matheny being marched off to his office for scolding on more than one occasion. I had a crush on Frankie for a while, but she was older and wiser than I was at the time. Mr. Gelling's good-manners policy carried over into evening movies, too. One night, he tracked down some popcorn-bag poppers and Coke-cup stompers that surprised him and everyone in the theatre. The guilty parties turned out to be the parents of a friend of mine. Mr. Gelling promptly marched them out of the theatre and booted them out of the Paramount. He was one vigilant man with a stern set of rules and a flawless memory. As I got older, I realized he was actually a very nice man. Riding herd on a house full of sugar-charged kids (or unruly adults) in a big dark room had to be danged near impossible—but he did it successfully. Rest in peace, Mr. Gelling.

When the Kiddie Show let out, kids were either picked up by parents or scattered throughout downtown in search of adventure. Some combination of Terry, Frank, David, Charlie, Wist, Clarence, Tuck and me usually headed straight for McClellan's or Woolworth to buy adventure "implements" to help us game our way through Saturday afternoon. The game was cops and robbers. Half of us bought water pistols and half of us bought peashooters and ammo. The "robbers" had five minutes to hide and then the "cops" came a huntin'. The mission was to sneak up on the enemy and pelt them with either water or peas. Blocks-long chases were commonplace, and it often took hours for one group to win. The peashooter guys usually ended up losing because they ran out of ammo and the water pistol guys could refill. To give credit where credit is due, it should be noted that Frank Timmins was the mastermind behind this game. He was creative that way. I will, however, now reveal that Frank's secret hiding place was a little, hard-to-get-to space between where the back of the Smith Furniture Store building joined the western side of the Hemingway Furniture building. Sorry, Frank, but the gig is up.

We usually played our way through downtown until we got hungry, ran out of money or began to get on each other's nerves and spats started to break out. Those three conditions usually set in about the same time, signaling us that it was time to head home.

Chapter 3
The Long Walk Home

As I left downtown and headed toward home on the Southside, I first passed Central Baptist Church, where I always made a quick visual search of the front yard for any money that may have fallen out of a church attendee's offering envelope. I conducted this search for cash because one time when Terry and I were walking to the Paramount, I found three half-dollars in front of the church. I never found any more money, but my good luck—or God's generosity—that day was burned into my brain.

Palace Dry Cleaning, which was owned by my classmate Susan Elliott's parents, was my next stop. I always tapped on the storefront window and waved at Mrs. Elliott, who was usually working the front counter. She never failed to return my wave and add a sweet smile. Next, I came to Sullivan's Funeral Home, with its two huge fir trees guarding its entrance. I always crossed the street to avoid walking too close to

Sullivan's because I knew it had a bunch of dead bodies lying inside. It gave me the creeps then and it still does today.

Next, I passed Applebaum's Scrap Yard. It was a massive scrap iron and metal yard, and I would sometimes stop and watch the cranes move the steel and iron from one pile to another or onto a waiting rail car. Even today, I can still catch the scent of rust, metal and diesel that used to ooze out of Applebaum's. Two of my first friends, the twins Diane and David Applebaum, were the children of Jack and Rosie Applebaum, owners of the scrap yard. They lived in an old, white, columned, two-story antebellum house right at the entrance to the junkyard. Whenever I visited David, we were allowed to play among the heaps of tangled metal, so long as we stayed away from the working machines. We usually played army, running from pile to pile shooting imaginary Germans by the thousands. We pretended the scrap piles were ruins from bombings. When we weren't fighting Nazis, a good deal of our time was spent trying to pry ball bearings out of things that had ball bearings in them. These ball bearings were better-known to us as "steelies," and they were highly-prized on the marble-shooting circuit. Today, when I stand where Applebaum's stood, the smell, the sounds and remembering the feel of the scrap metal bring a smile to my face, even though Applebaum's Scrap Yard, the Applebaum's big white house and my beloved friends David and Diane are now long gone.

Nowadays, when I close my eyes and step back into the '50s, another sound I hear is that of Hollywood mufflers bouncing their rumbles off our paved streets. If one was "into" cars and hot rods, "talkative" mufflers were a must. Each set of Hollywoods had their own sound, so we could generally tell who was coming toward us from blocks away because we recognized the car's "voice," Marshall in the '50s and '60s was full of Fonzies.

I guess every city in the world puts on its make-up and perfume when spring arrives and the brown grass greens up, the barren branches start blooming and the earth splits open with new flowers. I'll bet most all of us can recall the colors of our springs and the seasonal smells of our neighborhoods and hometowns. Our winters were usually relatively mild, and our soil was healthy and rich. We looked good in the springtime. We were—and still are, I hope—a town teeming with azaleas, camellias, roses and dogwoods, along with virtually all kinds of flowers. However, the smells of blooms that are most deeply seated in my memory bank are those from honeysuckle and wisteria. Seeing and sensing my hometown's immodest display of beauty during my walks home gave me comfort and deepened the pride I already felt.

We had a big gardenia bush in our side yard that smelled ultra-sweet. I wasn't crazy about its smell because I thought it smelled like Miss Yurek, a nice lady who worked at Sears with mother and always hugged me when I visited mom. She always had a gardenia pinned to her blouse or lapel, and it hit me right in the nose every time she hugged me. I liked her a lot, but enough of the sweet gardenia, already.

Since air conditioning didn't become a must-have for most families until the late 1950s, everyone left their windows open in hopes of catching a breeze. Attic fans were the cooler of choice in lots of home—including ours—and some of them were strong enough to suck the curtains off the windows. Each attic fan had its own unique "whomp" to it. The "whomp" was the sound made by the fan as it whirled around with its fan belt slightly slipping. The "whomp" became like a serenade that helped you fall asleep. When you slept somewhere other than your own home, you missed your "whomp." Even if the other house had an attic fan, no two "whomps" played the same tune.

Now, back to open windows. With the windows open, a walk through the neighborhood close to meal time offered strong clues as to what families were about to eat. Our neighborhood was big on fried chicken, chicken soup and ground beef cooked about every way imaginable so that's what most houses smelled like. Mother cooked and served lots of cabbage, so when she boiled it, I'm relatively certain the Ollers next door closed their windows. She also served us sauerkraut and weenies (a.k.a. wieners) fairly regularly, probably to the chagrin of the Ollers. By the way, does anyone building a house today put an attic fan in it? For that matter, does anyone still eat sauerkraut and weenies?

Like most towns and cities, Marshall was shaped by its diversity: black and white, rich and poor, erudite and ignorant, Republican and Democrat, the beautiful and the uglier than home-made soap, good folks and bad folks. There has long been a lot of oil and gas money in Marshall, but it never has managed to trickle down to the poor. As a kid, I informally defined wealth by whether or not a neighborhood had curbs, gutters and sometimes even sidewalks. South Grove Street, where we lived, was tarred and had ditches. That meant—to me—we were middle class. Two blocks north of us, the streets were dirt. They were poor. Understand my rating system? I will say that I do not recall much, if any, distinction being made between the different economic classes, at least among us kids. I had friends who lived in fine homes, and I had friends who lived on dirt streets. The few families in Marshall that appeared to be class-conscious were laughed at and made fun of behind their backs. Another class-defining thing was the kind of grass you had. Most wealthy folks had St. Augustine grass, while middle-class families got by with Bermuda. The poor had little or no grass.

Now and then, the city would re-tar a street in our neighborhood. Wet tar didn't keep us boys from crossing streets, so we tarred-up the bottoms of many pairs of sneakers, much to the chagrin of our parents. The pothole patching and re-tarring of your street made it look lots better and was a source of pride. It was also easier on your bicycle tires. When the new tar ran off into the ditches and got semi-hard, we would chew it like bubble gum. Our parents didn't discourage us from chewing tar because it was commonly believed it helped to clean the teeth. If there wasn't new tar to enjoy, there was always something else popping up to capture my interest, energy and imagination. I grew up thinking my house on South Grove Street was pretty much the center of the universe. As my walks home from downtown neared their end and home was in sight, I was happy. Every "long walk home" made new memories and stirred up old ones. Home was my starting place and my ending place for each day of adventure.

Chapter 4
The Cast of Characters

We moved from Marshall's East End to its Southside in 1948, so, naturally that's where I did most of my early growing up. Southside was a microcosm of greater Marshall in that it had all economic classes, housing that ranged from shacks to mansions and a raftload of characters who made living in Southside both interesting and challenging. Marshall was like that, too, and so were the Piney Woods of East Texas. One time I heard a fellow say Marshall was the home of "tall women and virgin pines." I don't remember the girls being particularly tall, but I do remember lots of pine trees, along with most of the details about growing up in what for me was a boy's version of adventure land.

I think my stories about growing up in Marshall in the 1950s will be more enjoyable if you know a bit about the characters with whom I was raised. Most of them will show up in one or more chapters. They are worth getting to know.

First of all, our neighborhood within Southside was essentially a five-block-by-five-block area filled with lots of boys and very, very few girls. The chart below illustrates my point:

FAMILY	#OF BOYS	# OF GIRLS
Eubanks	3	0
Weeks	2	0
Starke	2	0
Warnstaff	2	0
Reeves	2	0
Pace	1	0
Cole	3	0
Van Wert	3	1
Brassel	1	0
Van Reenan	2	0
Woods	2	1
Smith	2	0
Graham	2	0
Barrett	2	0
Galik	2	1
McClaran	1	1
Worley	1	1
Brown	1	1
Tamplin	3	0
Elliott	2	0
Pope	1	1
Waldrop	1	1
Morgan	1	1

York	0	2
Lea	1	3
Oller	0	1
Cargill	2	0
Black	2	0
Adams	1	1
Prothro	0	3
Lewandowski	1	0
Hynson	0	4
Schmidt	1	0
Williams	0	1
Williams	2	0
Miller	1	1
Magrill	1	1
Moore	3	1
Huntsberger	2	0
Padgett	1	1
Boyd	2	0
Hargiss	1	2
Fields	2	1
Stauts	2	1
Faust	1	2
Hall	1	0
Huffman	2	0
Furhh	2	0
Forsyth	1	0
Primo	3	0
Ford	2	0
Jenkins	2	0

Samson	1	0
Dixon	2	0
Faulkner	0	1
Schlitler	0	2
Martin	1	3
Totals	Boys: 85	Girls: 39

Get the picture? Playing sports, cowboys and Indians, cops and robbers and war were far more popular than playing dolls and tea parties in our neighborhood. Sally Van Wert was my best friend who was a girl. Sally quickly realized that if she wanted to be a "player," she had to learn to play war and the other boy-dominated games. She successfully made the transition and often showed up to play with her army helmet buckled on.

At one time or another, I did things with all of the kids counted in this chart—even the girls—and each contributed to the experience potion that became me. However, only a few play starring roles in my biography and you need to meet them. Say hello to:

Terry Weeks—Terry and I were best friends from age four on. We were the same age but, in most respects, that's where the similarities ended. I was tall and lanky; he was short and chubby. I had a long face; his was like one of those happy faces topped by a crew cut. I was fast; he wasn't. His dog, Dot, had long white hair, and my dog, Belle, had short black hair. Terry was cute; I wasn't. Every afternoon, Terry's mom gave him a sweet treat. It was sometimes a Popsicle, but his joy was eating Jell-O mix with a spoon. He was a sucker for anything red. Whether it was strawberry or cherry flavored, Terry loved it. And regardless of whether he had a Popsicle or a package of Jell-O mix, he always emerged from

School Days
1956-57

his break with a big red circle around his mouth. His red stain would stay in place until he had to go home at dark. Me? I preferred grape or lemon, but enjoying either flavor in the form of raw Jell-O didn't work for me. The differences went on and on, but despite all of them, we were best friends. We roomed together in college, plus we were each other's best man at our weddings (he got married on my wedding anniversary one year after I vowed-up). We were inseparable until our wives horned in on the action. But we're still best buds.

Charlie Starke—Charlie was smallish, quick, talented and cute as a bug. Not particularly gifted as a student or as an athlete, Charlie excelled at things like carving, drawing, putting model airplanes together with no glue showing and doing tricks with his yoyo. More importantly, Charlie could belch

29

SCHOOL DAYS
1957-58

or poot on command. Yes, I said "poot." The words "hell," "damn," "piss" and "fart" were considered to be cuss words, and we were not allowed to use them. Charlie was the perfect Cub and Boy Scout, and later an Eagle Scout. I was super jealous when he presented his carved deer head with antlers made from oak branches to our scoutmaster. Mine looked like a cross-eyed cow that had impaled his own head with briars. Charlie's was perfect. He was the kind of kid who looked good in a beanie. He also mastered the art of whistling loudly by holding two fingers to his lips in such a way that it amplified his whistle. I never learned how to do that, and, to this day, I suffer from "poor whistler's inferiority complex." Our friendship lasted through college, but it certainly had its ups and downs. I think we each secretly envied the other. I wished for his odd and arty skills, and I think he envied my athletic skills.

Clarence Warnstaff—Clarence was Charlie's best friend and they were inseparable just like Terry and me. Clarence giggled a lot, and when he got really tickled, he blew snot out of his nose. Despite this problem, Clarence always looked neat as a pin. He could crawl out of a ditch full of wet red clay and look like he was ready for church. It was like dirt didn't stick to him. He was into ham radioing, not sports. While Clarence and I never did a lot of stuff involving just the two of us, he was a full-fledged member of the street pack. He was voted "Most Handsome" in high school, and he deserved it.

David Reeves—From age five until he moved during the fourth grade, David was a close ally of Terry and me when it came to playing. His hair was jet black, and his eyes were a penetrating royal blue. All the mothers used to talk about how beautiful his eyes were. Handsome or not, David was slow to mature and had to repeat the first grade. He loved to play cowboys and Indians, and he always wanted to be Hopalong Cassidy. That

(L to R) David Reeves, Scotty Eubanks

was fine with Terry and me because Terry was Roy Rogers and I switched back and forth from being Gene Autry to being Lash LaRue. I was Lash when my brother Robert would let me play with his bullwhip. David and I packed a lot of memories into a short time.

Dickie Cole—Like me, Dickie was the youngest of three boys. His motor was always racing and keeping up with him was a four-star challenge. Building "huts" out of scrap lumber, cardboard, loose cinder blocks, etc., was very popular in our neighborhood and Dickie was by far considered the master builder. He even built multistory huts while the rest of us were

struggling just to get our four walls to stand up. He was also a good marbles player. He carried his marbles in a gutted ice tray. Dickie started working on cars when he was very young. He was a mechanical whiz and worked at Mr. Curtis's garage for more money at age nine than most of us made in high school. By the age of twelve, Dickie had moved on to Rayford's Garage where he became a top large-rig truck mechanic making adult mechanic's wages. He was a couple of years older than me, and because our mothers worked together at Sears & Roebuck and were good friends, I got a lot of his hand-me-down clothes. Most of the clothes were handed down to Dickie from his older brother John, who got the clothes handed down to *him* from his older brother Henry. By the time they made their way to my closet, Henry, John and

Dickie had about worn them threadbare. When I joined the Cub Scouts, Mrs. Cole gave me Dickie's old scout shirt, which had been John's before. It had been washed so many times it was light blue instead of the traditional dark blue. But it worked just fine and saved my family a little money. Dickie (now Dick) and I never let our friendship slip away, and we still talk to each other regularly. He parlayed his energy, industriousness and entrepreneurial skills into a sizable fortune. Even so, he never tried to be anyone other than Dickie Cole from the Southside of Marshall, Texas.

During the grade school years, I added four close and lifelong buddies from outside my neighborhood who became major players in my "wonder years." They were all Southsiders, just not from my immediate neighborhood. Let me introduce them to you:

David Wist—Wist (he went by "Wist," not David, most of the time) and I really kicked off our friendship in the third grade. He quickly established himself as a friend I could count on, regardless of the situation. He soon became a frequent visitor to my house, with the frequency reaching its apex in high school but it continues even today. He was exceptionally bright, scoring in the top 1 percent nationally on any and all of the aptitude tests given to students. As bright as he was, he was well behind many of us on the "street smarts" scale. He was, however, a quick learner and stepped up his game with relative ease. Our mutual interests in smoking, gambling, the St. Louis Cardinals and Carol Marshall sort of bound us together from age eight on. Our relationship hit a rough spot in the seventh grade when Carol dumped me in favor of Wist—a move I still can't figure out. If we had given Wist a nickname in junior or senior high, it would have been "Sleepy." He simply could not stay awake in class, when he visited a friend or when we went riding around looking for girls. His propensity to sleep was finally diagnosed as narcolepsy, but not until he was well into his adult years. In retrospect, if he hadn't been so smart, he would not have been able to make "A"s, graduate from the University of Texas or excel as a professional in the computer field. As this saga I'm penning continues into my junior high and high school years, Wist takes on a larger and larger role. We shared some wild and darn near incredible adventures together.

Frank Timmins—Frank became a friend early during our first-grade year. He quickly showed himself to be a better-than-average playground athlete. He could catch, hit and throw at a time when most of the other kids were really struggling with the very basics of all things athletic. I will, however, say that it was Frank's interest in pranksterism I remember most about him. He had a twinkle in his eye that left no doubt that he was up for any kind of hijinks you could dream up. Water guns, pea shooters, spit wads, water balloons, cherry bombs and whoopee cushions were all right up his alley. If you liked mischief, you'd have been well-advised to hang close to Frank.

If Frank wasn't involved in some form of mischief, he was just in the process of dreaming up his next caper.

Once, in the early evening, Frank, Terry and I decided to hide in a row of elm trees along Bomar Street and bomb cars with water balloons as they zipped by. Terry had a tough time hitting the cars, but Frank and I were good at it. Unfortunately, we weren't good at screening the cars we blasted, and we "successfully" nailed a police patrol car. The police car stopped abruptly, and the two policemen jumped out of their car and nabbed Frank. Terry and I had made a clean get-away but Frank just froze. The police shined their flashlight in Frank's face and asked him what he was doing. Frank just started caressing the elm tree he was hiding behind and stared intently at its bark. He then answered, "I was just petting the tree." The policemen looked at each other, shook their heads, and told Frank to burst the rest of his balloons and get his butt home. While Frank's answer wouldn't have earned him an Oscar, it did work with Marshall's finest. Hmmm.

Frank often invited one or two friends to spend the night with him on Friday nights. Quite often—right before bedtime—Frank would sneak off and cover his face and high forehead with flour, turn off his bedroom lights and hide on the far side of his bed. When you entered the room, he would shine a flashlight under his chin, spring from behind the bed and let out a blood-curdling screech. The eeriness of the lighted flour on his face, the frightening noise and the surprise of it all just plain scared the dickens out of any and all of us. His antics always made for an interesting evening. It should also be noted that whatever we were doing on the Friday night would be interrupted when the Friday Night Fights, sponsored by Gillette, came on television. Frank's dad, Amos, would without fail yell, "Frankie Boy, ya'll get in here and watch the fights!" It wasn't an invitation. It was an order; so we watched. Mr. Amos usually lay on his sofa and watched Gene Fullmer whip Carmen Basilio for the umpteenth time while he ate a gallon of raw oysters. Frank was—and still is—my friend.

Tuck Kemper—Although Tuck and I started the first grade together, our friendship didn't fully blossom until about the third or fourth grade. Tuck was a Southsider, but his house was a good ten or twelve long blocks from my house. I occasionally rode my bike over to his house, but he wasn't allowed to cross Washington Street on his own. So when he came to play at my house, his mom had to drive him over. I and most of my friends could, at times, be jerks and rather tough to get along with. Not Tuck. He was easy to get along with and always seemed to go out of his way to be a people pleaser. Maybe that's why he became an Air Force chaplain and later a missionary. Much of our early comradery developed out of our mutual passion for sports, particularly baseball and football. When sides were chosen for teams during recess, Tuck was always in the top four or five. In junior high, I was the starting left halfback, and Tuck was my back up. Early in the season, a defensive end from Carthage, Texas, named Mike Screws (I'm not making that name up) put a vicious tackle on me and broke all of the ribs on my right side. The next day, our local newspaper's article about our 20–6 loss to Carthage carried the headline, "Carthage Puts Screws to Eubanks, Wins 20–6." Clever, huh? Our volunteer team doctor was Tuck's dad, a prominent local obstetrician-gynecologist. My injury made Tuck the starting left halfback and made me the only football player in Texas who was being treated for his macho injury by a gynecologist. Tuck fumbled a lot, and I was mortified more than once at being the only guy sitting in a waiting room full of women to see their gynecologist. You could say we both suffered from my injury.

I figured Tuck was one of my richest friends—not because he flaunted his money or because he or his family acted rich—but because he was my only friend whose family had a refrigerator full of Coca-Cola. My family and the families of the rest of my friends considered soft drinks to be an expensive luxury and just didn't have them. The Kempers not only had Cokes in their "ice box," they had cases of them stacked up in their garage! Tuck, his mother and daddy, his two sisters, Sue and Kathy, and his little brother Jerry all sort of felt like family to me. Good folks. Tuck and I went all through college together, and our bond of friendship remains strong today.

David Applebaum—I mentioned David and his twin sister Diane earlier. It should come as no surprise to learn that

David's nickname was "Apple." Sometimes, when Apple had done something noteworthy, we called him "A-Bomb." We were a clever lot, don't you think? David and his twin sister Diane started first grade with me in Mrs. Robbins's class. David and I hit it off immediately, and I frequently walked home with him and Diane after school. As I mentioned, they lived in a big, white antebellum home that was on the grounds of Applebaum's Scrap Iron and Metal Company, a large operation the family owned and operated. Our after-school walks to their house took us by a low-lying, tree-covered vacant lot on Pecan Street on which folks dumped the autumn leaves they had raked from their nearby yards. One afternoon, a raker had made a big, new pile of leaves that just begged me to jump into it. Recognizing an opportunity to show off in front of Diane, I implored them to watch me as I made a mad dash for the leaf pile. When I reached the pile, I dove head first into it, planning to emerge from the other end to their applause, giggles and nods of admiration. Unbeknown to me, there was a stump hidden under the leaves. With a full head of steam, I slid on my belly into the stump face first. After a moment of head clearing and eye refocusing, I emerged from the leaf pile screaming at the top of my lungs and bleeding like a stuck hog from the face. We all ran like crazy to the Applebaum's house where Mrs. Applebaum drove me to the doctor's office for repairs. Mother met us there and watched as Dr. Heidelberg stitched up my nose, upper and lower lips and chin. No one was impressed by my daring leaf-leap, but Diane and David were goggle-eyed at my twenty-one stitches.

David, a.k.a. "Apple," had some athletic ability, but when the rest of us started growing, he was stuck in pee-wee size and just couldn't keep up with the rest of us. His parents fretted over his smallness and took him to Dallas to see a doctor who specialized in growth issues. Nothing they did seemed to help, but when David reached high school, he shot up to around six foot tall. We went off to college together, and he was quite the hit with all the girls. He was tall, handsome and a danged fine young man. He was my friend.

If there was a nicer family in Marshall than the Applebaums, I never met them. Today, I not only miss David and Diane, I miss their mom and dad, Miss Rosie and Mr. Jack.

Many friends beyond those I've described here played pivotal roles in my life from my pre-school years through elementary school. Johnny Galik, Richard Magrill, Scooter Adams, Jimmy Elliott and Dickie Brassell were gold-star friends, but those herein written about were the super stars. Most are still alive, some are not; but every one of them is fully alive inside of me and romps freely through my memories on a regular basis.

Chapter 5
Our House on South Grove Street

Growing up in Marshall, Texas, in the 1950s had its minuses, but I was never daunted by them—I was aware of them, to be sure, but never daunted by them. Oh, I still remember how poverty, alcohol abuse, racial tensions and mental illness affected many households, but the passage of time has purged most of the gray memories from my data bank, and they are not the subjects of this particular literary effort.

We lived on South Grove Street in Marshall's Southside, and the houses in our neighborhood were mostly small, two-bedrooms, one-bath houses built right after World War II to accommodate returning veterans. Such was the case with our house. It was nine-hundred square feet. Today, I realize it was small, but that fact never crossed my mind when I was living there. We were a solid family unit, so lots of good stuff went on in that little frame house. All my friends and those of my brothers seemed to enjoy hanging out there, too. The welcome mat was always out, and friends and visitors had no trouble slipping right into our lifestyle. Our house had good vibes.

My two older brothers, Homer and Robert, and I not only shared a bedroom, we shared a bed. Being the youngest, I had to sleep in the middle, so each night, I had to survive flying elbows, knee jabs and vile gas clouds that came at me in full stereo. Our diets included lots of eggs, baloney (bologna) and tons of pinto beans. I loved all of those things, but now I realize what a price they extracted from me each night when they fueled those butt-launched death grenades that often brought tears to my eyes. Even so, I recall many nights when the three of us boys laid in bed laughing uncontrollably, finally drifting off to sleep with arms, legs and smiles happily intertwined.

In our house, Daddy was in charge. My brothers and I never, ever forgot who ran the show. He believed boys needed a broad range of experiences if they were to grow up to become well-rounded men, so we were given lots of free rein in our doings. However, there were rules and we knew what they were and that our failure to follow them inevitably led to a session with Daddy. Not a good thing. He wasn't above spanking us, and had done so numerous times. However, he seldom had to resort to physical punishment. That man could

25

give you a look that stopped just short of breaking bones and scored a ten on the fright scale. Even today, the memory of Daddy's "oh hell" look causes my scalp to peel back and the hair on the back of my neck to stand up. One time when he had a case of the reds over something I had done, he told me, "Son, you do that again and I'll make you go catch something wild!" I had no idea what that meant, but I knew I wanted nothing to do with such an assignment.

Like so many of the dads at that time in America, Daddy had gone to war and come back with a few internal scars. By no means was he a basket case, and he had emerged from the experience ebullient with the victory, proud of his service and filled with optimism for the future. But he seemed to come back thirstier than he had been pre-war. He gravitated toward the American Legion where he and lots of other veterans would sit around talking about the war over a few—sometimes many—Budweisers or shots of Early Times. Sometimes, he and his cronies would emerge from a hard night of "warring" and drinking and surprise Mother and us boys with a late-night visit to our house where they could continue their talking while Mother made breakfast for all of them. On such evenings, none of them should have been driving, but they all did and their attempts at parking in front of our house left their cars looking like the bumper cars at an amusement park when the ride was over. Quite often, the vets suffering the most from too much of a good thing got a free ride home from Mother or my oldest brother, Homer. I woke up many mornings with Mr. Davenport's Ford and Mr. Pollack's maroon Kaiser sitting in front of our house. They were always picked up by noon. I learned a lot about the war by listening in on those discussions. I also learned the names of the local men who always checked in to the hospital when there was a draft call. These men weren't invited to breakfast at our house.

Daddy was a bit of a character. He was decisive, a man of action. Mother was always on his case about dropping cigarette ashes on the large green rug in our living room. Tired of her riding him about the ashes, he came up with a solution. One day, while Mother was at work, Daddy had our green rug replaced with a new gray one. When Mother got home and stared unbelievingly at the new rug, Daddy said, "Now, Zee, find those damn ashes!"

Some men have the perceived ability to drink themselves handsome and suave; some drink themselves tough; and some drink themselves smart. Daddy drank himself wealthy. One time, when he was in a "wealthy" state of mind, he bought a 21-inch Zenith television. It came in a huge cabinet and, more importantly, it was the first television in our neighborhood. Folks from as far away as four or five blocks came by to stare at it. The first television show I remember seeing was a Western serial named *The Three Mesquiteers* (an obvious take-off on Dumas's *The Three* Musketeers) starring Bob Steele. As I recall, Steele's white hat was about as big as he was. However, regardless of what show was on, every kid in the neighborhood regularly took root on our living room floor, and we all sat staring at ghostly images moving around in a field of electronic snow. Early one morning, my friend Dickie Cole came over to watch TV. It was so early, programming had not begun, so he and I watched the test pattern for over an hour. For those of you too young to know what a test pattern was, it was a geometric figure that came on the screen an hour before programming began. It just sat there, staring back at the big-eyed kids staring at it. By the way, Mother was not at all happy with Daddy's extravagance, but it was done, and the television was there to stay.

My favorite shows were *Howdy Doody* and *Pinkie Lee*, which followed Howdy and the gang. My brothers, who were teenagers at the time, liked *The Hit Parade*, starring Gisele MacKenzie, Dorothy Collins, Snookie Lanson and Russell Arms. Daddy owned the Zenith on Wednesday nights and Friday nights when boxing was on. We all conceded the TV to Mother when it was time for *The Lawrence Welk Show*. We all dug the *Ed Sullivan Show* on Sunday nights.

Terry Weeks's family was next to get a television. One time Terry became frustrated when he couldn't tune the snow out of *Sky King* and he kicked the screen. It was an ineffectual solution, as the snow persisted and the screen now had a big crack than ran top to bottom. When Mr. Weeks got home from work, Terry was grounded for an extended period of time.

Television changed us all. Some kids quit playing outside, and the need to use one's imagination seemed less important now that we could hitch a ride on someone else's by watching television.

Holidays were spectacular at our house. When we hosted at Thanksgiving or Christmas, aunts, uncles and cousins poured in from all over East Texas and parts of Louisiana. There would often be fifty to sixty folks show up and they

Scotty and cousins (listed in descending order)
Mary Ellen, Millie, Sandy and Becky at small family reunion.

all brought food or gifts, depending on which holiday it was. Daddy would round up a bunch of saw horses and lay plywood sheets on top of them and virtually cover our backyard with impromptu tables. I don't ever remember it raining on such days.

Regardless of whether it was Thanksgiving or Christmas, cousins Randy and Gary, who lived in New Boston, Texas, always brought firecrackers, mostly Black Cats and cherry bombs. As soon as they arrived, the search was on for things to blow up. Tin cans and stray cats were the most highly-prized targets. One time, Randy and my brother Robert found a bird's nest in the hollow pipe that was the top part of our clothes line pole. They set off a string of Black Cats in one end of it and blew birds, feathers, parts of their nest and an abandoned wasp nest out the other end. Believe it or not, two sparrows that were home at the time of the blitzkrieg stumbled around a bit and managed to fly off to the safety of our chinaberry tree. I don't know where those birds ended up, but I can guarantee you they went through the rest of their lives deaf and cross-eyed. The adult women were really hacked off at Randy and Robert and confiscated the rest of their ammo.

Christmas was special because back then everyone gave gifts to everyone else. Aunt Mary went on all the kids' black list when one year she introduced the concept of drawing names for gift giving. But we got over it. Another thing that made

Christmas special was the once-a-year visit from Mother's parents, Lee and Josie Chance; or Daddy Chance and Momma Chance to us grandkids. They owned and operated the V Inn Bar and Café in Alexandria, Louisiana. It wasn't exactly the Ritz—a pretty rough joint, in fact. Daddy Chance was iconic to us kids because for much of his life he was a professional gambler, and he always slept with a loaded pistol under his pillow. When working at his bar, he kept it tucked under his belt with the handle showing to warn off those who may be up to no good. He once won a Coca-Cola bottling plant in a poker game. His brother ran it for a while but Daddy Chance later traded it for a saw mill and quite a few acres of timber land. Usually on Christmas Eve, Momma and Daddy Chance would ride the train from Alexandria to Marshall. Everyone was glad to see them, but perhaps none more than the adult men of the family. You see, Daddy Chance always brought each man a fifth of whiskey concealed in a brown paper sack. Like little boys hiding their toys, the men would take their joy juice straight to our garage and find just the right spot for it. By late afternoon, the men had stopped sneaking into the garage for a snort and were all openly gathered in the back of the garage taking frequent hits on their brown paper bags. By this time, the women were in the kitchen cleaning up and working up a group mad at the men for what they were doing in the garage. This scene repeated itself every Christmas for many years.

Our house on South Grove Street was the center of my universe until I was fifteen, when we moved to a bigger, nicer house in another part of South Marshall. Our house on South Grove was a true home. It was filled with love and laughter and life. I've joyously carried those memories from that house with me everywhere I've been. They have always served me well.

Chapter 6
And We Played War, Cowboys, Baseball, and Other Stuff

In the early 1950s, I suppose most young boys in America spent considerable time playing war. I feel safe in saying far more German and Japanese soldiers "died" on the playgrounds and in the backyards of America than in the real war. Heck, on a good afternoon, Terry and I killed several hundred in my yard alone. It was amazing how many times we were thrust into hand-to-hand combat situations that inevitably led to "air" wrestling with the enemy. Though wounded countless times, I'm proud to say I never lost a one-on-one battle with bayonet-wielding Japanese or Lugar-toting Germans. Foxholes were absolutely essential to a good war game. Most of the vacant lots in the neighborhood were generously dotted with these war holes, but sometimes the press of battle required

Scotty (L) and Charlie (R) are armed for war.
Thousands would die at their hands.

us to dig one in someone's yard. Doing so seldom pleased the homeowner. I will always remember the anger etched on Mr. Weeks's face when he got home from work one day to find Terry and me lobbing hand grenades from a foxhole we had just dug in the middle of a patch of St. Augustine grass he had being babying along for months. War is hell, and, on that day, so was Mr. Weeks.

The main gathering place for neighborhood boys looking to meet up with other boys to play with was The Lot. The Lot was about four contiguous vacant lots the dads and older boys of the neighborhood kept mowed for us to play on. It was primarily a baseball field, but it was big enough to accommodate hut cities, war games and anything else our imaginations could dream up. The Lot was so popular and drew so many boys, the local electric utility had a crew build us a professional backstop for our ball diamond. They "planted" six tall utility poles and strung them with chicken wire. It was first class and, for the most part, kept our foul balls from flying onto Bomar Street or Medill Street.

In deep, deep left field and left-center field, twenty to thirty of us had dotted the landscape with strategically located foxholes and trenches to replicate a battlefield as best we could. Some were connected to other foxholes by tunnels. The tunnels were, in fact, ditches with the tops covered by plywood sheets that were then covered by dirt. Most of our bunkers had "secret" compartments dug into the side walls. These compartments were, in fact, ammo dumps because they were filled with dirt clods (grenades) for use during battles with opposing armies. The main problem with our war games was that no one wanted to be the enemy. We were all American soldiers so it was hard to scare up a battle. Quite often, the game of war was put aside and a good old dirt clod fight broke out. Inevitably, someone would run out of clods and start chunking rocks. Once this happened, all hell broke loose and those with few or no rocks would rush the better-armed foxholes. The older boys had a distinct advantage over the younger boys, who usually ended up heading for home in full retreat. Dickie Cole, who was two or three years older than me, had the best-built and best-armed foxhole. Since we were good pals, I usually took refuge in his foxhole. I'm sure I was a pain in the butt to Dickie, but I'm still grateful to him for saving me from the savagery of the rock-hurling Dickie Brassell.

The victory over the Axis powers painted every aspect of life in our country with a brush dripping with relief, euphoria, optimism and feelings of invincibility. Those feelings even leeched their way down to us kids. Many of the moms of those of us whose dads had served during the war cut down and altered the uniforms our dads brought home so they fit us mini-soldiers. My dad had served in the Navy, so my jumping in and out of foxholes on the battlefields of South Marshall wearing Navy whites sort of strained credulity. No problem, though. I was one fierce warrior, and quite proud of my uniform.

Sally Van Wert was the only girl who regularly came to The Lot to play war. She would show up wearing a real Army helmet that swallowed her tiny head. She would timidly stand at the edge of the "battlefield" hoping to be invited to play. Inevitably, someone was short of soldiers and would invite Sally to jump in. She then would eagerly run into the war arena with her helmet bouncing all over her head and

Terry, Scotty and Sally Van Wert (L to R),
three long-time amigos indulging their imaginations.

face. While her grenade-throwing arm was a bit weak, she
was strong on courage and would stand side-by-side with the
boys as the grenades flew. Her helmet came in handy more
than once. She was a real trooper.

My Uncle Whitey had served in the South Pacific and
had brought home some victory spoils. He gave our family
two spectacular Japanese officer swords. I wasn't allowed to
play with them, which was okay with me because they were
too long and too heavy for me to manage. My older brothers, Homer and Robert, however, could "duel" with them.
One time, Robert and John Cole were dancing around in our

front yard with the swords when the harmless blade clanging started getting out of hand. Both teens started getting red-faced and the clanging got harder and harder. They were just seconds away from starting to lunge and thrust when my oldest brother, Homer, stopped the battle. After that, the swords were off-limits to all of us.

Like any other neighborhood game, the popularity of playing war ran in spurts. One week it was war, the next week it was baseball, and then it was marbles, yo-yos, or spinning tops. However, when *To Hell and Back*—the movie about Audie Murphy's incredible war heroics and starring him—came out, playing war experienced a revival that lasted a long time. The unforgettable scene of Audie standing on a tank and mowing down countless Germans with a machine gun led to many, many dented hoods in the driveways of Marshall and, I suspect, all over America. Since tanks were scarce in our neighborhood, young infantrymen had no choice but to jump on car hoods from which they held off hundreds of charging German soldiers. The movie really resonated with the boys in Texas because Audie—like us—hailed from the Lone Star State.

We played more than war. I, along with most of the other younger kids, was really into playing cowboys and Indians. In truth, we usually just played cowboys because we spent far more time corralling train robbers and cattle rustlers than we did fighting renegades or Geronimo. Images of cowboy heroes like Roy Rogers, Gene Autry and Hopalong Cassidy—the big three of cowboydom—adorned everything from lunch boxes to cap pistols and holsters, to comic books and movie posters. Every kid in America knew who they were. There were a whole lot of arguments among friends over who would get to be Roy or who would get to be Gene when it came time to ride off in search of bad guys. Terry always wanted to be Roy Rogers, and David always wanted to be Hopalong. That was fine with me because I always wanted to be Gene Autry or Lash LaRue, depending on which horse I was riding that day and whether brother Robert would let me play with his whip that day. Lash always wore black, rode a black horse, and was a magician with a whip. The Lone Ranger was sort of popular, too. However, no one ever wanted to be the Lone Ranger because it was too hot and humid in Marshall to wear a black mask, and also you couldn't get anyone to "be" his trusty sidekick Tonto. We were all stars, not sidekicks.

None of us had "store bought" stick horses. Brooms that had been discarded by our moms became our horses. The straw part of the broom was the head of the horse, and when we galloped off in search of evildoers, we grabbed a handful of straw (the mane), straddled the stick and took off to enforce justice. Mother went through a lot of brooms so I had a sizable stable. Most of the brooms had yellow (palomino) or red (roan) sticks, but I had one black stick broom.

When I saddled up the black broom, I was Lash LaRue. It just wouldn't have been right to put Gene Autry on a black horse or Lash LaRue on a palomino. Terry was chubby and slow. David was just slow. I could run fast, so, therefore, I had the fastest horses. Terry and David just thought their moms had bought slower brooms than had my mother. When riding our horses, we would drag the end of the stick in the dust, thus kicking up dust just like Trigger, Champion and Topper did in the movies. We put a lot of fun miles on our "horses," and I absolutely hated it when we reached the age when riding broomstick horses made us look stupid to the older kids.

Sports were the other major-league pastimes for the boys of our neighborhood. In the spring and summer, baseball was our passion. In the fall and winter, it was football. On a nice summer day, as many as fifteen or twenty boys would show up at The Lot for a pick-up game of baseball. Most of those reporting for duty were between the ages of twelve and sixteen, but I started being allowed to play from the age of six. I was the only "little" kid who knew the rules and could catch, throw and hit. By the time I was eight, I was no longer the last kid chosen when sides were picked. All modesty aside, I was a very good athlete and my skillset offset my lack of years. Gene Samson was the best hitter at The Lot. He was one of the older kids, but, even so, his power to right field was legendary in South Marshall. Gene's stardom took a real hit when local developer (my cousin by marriage) Buster Rauschek built a duplex in deep right field, and we had to create a rule that said if you hit a ball into right field, you were out. Gene couldn't hit to left or center so he "retired" from The Lot at about age fifteen. Other good hitters were Charlie Pace, who went by the nickname "Funny," and Bill Huntsburger. One time Bill was playing center field and "Funny" launched a long fly ball to deep, deep center. Bill tore out running, watching the mammoth hit over his shoulder. We were all watching this drama unfold when, all of a sudden, Bill vanished. He had fallen in Dickie Cole's big, deep foxhole. Finally, Bill crawled out of the foxhole all bruised, scratched and limping. He just waved at everyone and limped on home. "Funny" was awarded a home run and the game continued, minus Bill Huntsburger, of course. It should be noted there were so many rocks on the field at The Lot that sliding wasn't really popular. Also, ground balls tended to bounce in all directions off the rocks. We would have rock-picking sessions pretty regularly, but it didn't seem to do any good. When we came back the next day, after hauling off loads and loads of rocks the day before, there would be more rocks than we started with. Ebb Stark told me the rocks bred during the night, giving birth to more rocks each night. It made sense to me, and I believed him until I was about twelve.

Most of our playing at The Lot occurred during summer. It was as hot as blazes, but about the only thing that could break up our game or battle was the sound of the ice cream truck as it neared The Lot. The sound of that truck caused everything to go into freeze-frame. The first thing everyone did was to inventory his available cash in hopes he had enough for a popsicle or some other treat. Those who did have enough money would stand by the edge of the street and frantically wave the truck down. Those who didn't have the money usually made a mad dash home in hopes of getting a parent to quickly fork over some change. A lot of parents said no, and a lot of parents dilly-dallied so long, the truck was gone by the time they returned. I remember one time when one of the boys jumped onto the truck's back bumper as it pulled away. He then opened the door to the refrigerated compartment and started throwing frozen goodies out behind the truck. I got a fudgesicle from his loot and he was my hero for the rest of the afternoon. I'm not totally sure who that Robin Hood was, but I think it was Dickie Brassell. He might deny it today, but I think it was him.

We also occasionally used deep left and deep center fields to build hut cities. It was popular in the '50s to round up scrap lumber, odd pieces of tin, bricks, cardboard, etc., and use it all to build huts. Sometimes, enough kids built huts to where we would have twelve to twenty huts, or a hut city. Each builder tried to outdo the other builders so some of the huts got quite fancy. Finding building materials often got rather aggressive, and, quite often, they ended up being "borrowed" from construction sites or some unknowing neighbor's garage. I remember one time when Mr. Crudup

(L to R) Donald Smith, John Cole, Charlie "Funny" Pace with Terry Weeks on his back, David Reeves, Dickie Cole, Gaines Weeks and Steve Reeves hangin' out in Hut City which was built in center field at The Lot.

came to Hut City and disassembled Ebb and Charlie Stark's hut, thus reclaiming all the stuff they had taken from his backyard. Dickie Cole was the master hut builder, having one time built a three-story hut with a dumb waiter in it. Dickie's ability to convert trash into building supplies was remarkable. His ability to pilfer building supplies from unsuspecting neighbors was also remarkable.

One time, Terry, Charlie and I decided to build a hut but could only scrounge enough materials to build two walls. I came up with a solution that made sense to me. We decided to build it in my backyard, using the side of the concrete steps that came from our kitchen door to the yard as one wall and the exterior of the house as another wall. By nestling our hut into the area where the steps met the wall of the house, we eliminated the need to build two of the four walls. We added the other two walls, and voila—we had a hut. Daddy and my two older brothers had finished painting our frame house white and our back steps red the week before, so two of our interior walls looked great. The two walls we constructed were mostly cardboard. They weren't pretty, but they sufficed. We played there most of the day and then, well, we got bored. We were only five or six years old but we quickly agreed on what would be fun. We decided to set our hut on fire. We did, and things got ugly fast. Flames and black smoke started shooting up the back of our house. Mother's kitchen window was right above our hut, and, thank God, she saw the flames and smoke dancing in front of her eyes. She quickly darted out the back door, grabbed the water hose and turned it on our flaming hut. Her quick reaction averted a giant disaster and saved me from facing capital punishment at the hands of "Judge" Daddy. The fire raised blisters on the new paint job and turned a large swath of it black. Daddy, Homer and Robert had to sand it down and repaint it. It wasn't my proudest moment, but the trauma it inflicted on me ended my experimentation with arson.

I did, however, watch a fire every now and then. One year, a few days after Christmas, the Weeks and the Coles both threw their discarded Christmas trees in the big ditch that ran behind their houses. The fir trees had spent their juices on Christmas and were dried to the bone. I might add, the grass in the ditch was as dry as the trees because, after all, it was winter. I was sitting on my living room floor playing with my toy soldiers when I heard a scream that was shot through with panic. I ran to the front yard, which was across from the ditch where the two families had thrown their trees. The

Little Dickie Cole, always on the edge of mischief.

ditch was on fire, and it was spreading fast! The screamer was my friend Dickie Cole, who was running all around and hollering for somebody—anybody—to get a hose. Apparently, Dickie hadn't been able to come up with anything to do, so he decided to burn the old Christmas trees. They went from being lit to burning out of control in three seconds flat. The fire was marching toward the Weeks house, the Cole house and the Pace house like it was running late. Finally, enough neighbors collectively brought the "Great Marshall Fire" under control. Dickie's eyes remained as big as saucers for a couple of days, but he eventually settled down and got back to being Dickie.

Each holiday season, someone in our neighborhood got hold of some fireworks. One July 4th, Terry and I got hold of a bunch of Black Cat firecrackers and dedicated the afternoon to blowing up stuff. We soon tired of blowing up bottles, cans and toy soldiers, and decided to climb up on the roof of his garage. It was tin and had a severely sloped pitch. When we precariously balanced ourselves on the roof, we began to light and throw the firecrackers off the roof onto the imaginary storming Japanese army below. We had successfully fought the Japanese soldiers off for several intense minutes when one of the Black Cats "fast-burned" and blew up in my hand. The explosion scared me, hurt me, and, perhaps worst of all, caused me to lose my balance and roll off the roof onto the hard ground below. Despite being addled by the fall and hurting like the dickens from the explosion, I tore off for home for consolation and medical attention. My parents soaked my hand in coal oil and then wrapped it in ice. When I told Daddy how it had happened, he patted me on top of my head and told me I had become a casualty of war.

About a year after the new duplex encroached significantly on our right field, a church was built in deep left field. While I never doubted God loved "the little children," it became clear that not all of God's people felt the same way, particularly when the children were knocking baseballs onto their roof and through their windows. The arrival of a duplex and God to our Lot, coupled with the aging of our neighborhood's crop of boys, spelled the end of The Lot as our gathering spot. It was, in my mind, the perfect park. It was a blank canvas on which we could put our imaginations to work and see our dreams take shape. Every neighborhood needs such a place as The Lot.

Once in a while, Dickie Brassell, who was a year older than me, would wander down to my house. Our efforts to play together usually ended up in a squabble or a fight. For some reason, most of our fights ended up as rock fights. He would feign going home and usually stop across the street in the Reeves's rock-filled driveway and start sailing rocks at me. He probably wasn't a better rock thrower than me, but he was definitely better at picking battle sites than me. By standing

Scotty (L) and Dickie Brassell (R) enjoying each other's company before a rock fight breaks out.

in the Reeves's driveway, he had taken the higher ground and his site had an endless supply of ammo. He was left handed and had a knack for picking flat rocks that he could curve right into me. My driveway, yard and the ditch in front of our house had very few rocks, so I was badly undergunned. Plus, I was always throwing uphill. My situation usually resulted in me charging Dickie in hopes of moving the fight from rocks to wrestling. My aggression usually ended up with him highballing it to his house in full retreat. He had won the rock fight, but, in the end, I had reclaimed my turf. Dickie and I ended up playing high school baseball together. I was the shortstop and he was—as you might have guessed—a better than average, side-arming curve ball pitcher. Rock fighting wasn't really a game we played; it was just spontaneous chaos that seemed to break out when Dickie and I spent too much time together.

From the first grade through about the fourth grade, we played a lot of marbles. Bull's Eye was a favorite. Each player put some marbles in the center of a big circle. If you knocked a marble out of the circle, you got to keep it, assuming, of course, you were playing "keepsies" and not "funsies." However, our main game was Cat's Eye. In Cat's Eye, you drew an eye in the dirt and lined up about eight marbles in a straight line inside the eye. The object was to knock one marble at a time out of the eye, and you got to keep any that cleared the eye. All of the games had strict rules that were sternly enforced.

We all played "keepsies," meaning you didn't return your friend's marbles at the end of the game. Good shooters ended up amassing marble fortunes over time. My "fortune" got a nice boost when Dickie got too old to play marbles and gave me his marbles, which he kept in an old ice tray. I won lots of marbles in the 1950s, all of which I still have. They reside in six quart-sized, glass-topped, Mason fruit jars.

At the beginning of each school year, yo-yos went through a month or two of popularity. Yo-yo mania peaked each year when Duncan Yo-Yos, the leaders in yo-yo production, sent a master yo-yoer around to the neighborhood grocery stores that sold their products to demonstrate all the incredible tricks you could do with a yo-yo. The demos worked. We bought the dickens out of yo-yos and were convinced we could become overnight experts that would amaze our friends at school the next day. Charlie Stark and Maner Jones got pretty good at yo-yoing, but most of us just did vanilla yo-yoing. Honestly, yo-yoing never held my interest. For one thing, standing around yo-yoing just didn't make sense to me and was kind of boring. The second reason I didn't get into it was because I wasn't any good at it.

I think the season for playing with spinning tops followed right on the heels of yo-yo season. The tops I'm talking about were the kind that fit in your palm and you wrapped string around them. You then threw them down, and the uncoiling of the string caused the top to spin for quite a while. "Topping" required some skill, and successful spins required good string wrapping and the right throwing technique. Very few boys got good at top throwing. I did. The only game we ever played with tops was Bustem. In Bustem, when you were the buster, you tried to make the metal tip of your top hit the top of your opponent's top with such force that it split it open. Since the tops of the 1950s were wooden, they *would* split if they were hit on the "sweet spot." To gain an edge, it was common practice among Bustem players to sharpen the tips of their throwin' tops to make them more deadly. In truth, very few top fatalities occurred in our Bustem games. A direct hit on someone's toe was more likely to happen than one's top scoring a lethal blow on someone else's top.

We commonly played outside from sunup until sundown. Because Marshall got forty-six inches of rain a year and was horribly humid, the mosquitoes thrived there and drove everyone nuts. In an effort to improve its citizens' quality of life, the City of Marshall sent fogging trucks throughout the neighborhoods on a regular basis during the summer. The trucks sprayed a continuous, thick, white cloud made from atomizing DDT and other drugs that were toxic to the mosquitoes. When the fogging truck hit your neighborhood, it served as a call to action for all who had bicycles. It was great sport to ride right behind the truck where the cloud of deadly chemicals was the thickest, and follow the truck for three or four blocks. While it's no telling what harm we did to ourselves inhaling that crap, no one died on the spot. We stunk for several hours, but, as I said, no one died. I might also add, we suffered no mosquito bites the rest of the day.

Since we often played into the evening, mothers had different ways to signal their child when it was time to come home. My mother whistled sharply three times to tell me to come in for the night. Mrs. Weeks and Mrs. Starke used plastic whistles with peas inside of them to signal to Terry and Charlie that the fun was over. Each of them blew their whistle a certain way that allowed each boy to know when the whistle was for him. It was a pretty good system until Dickie Cole got his hands on a whistle. Dickie learned to mimic Mrs. Weeks's coded whistle and used it repeatedly to confuse Terry. Dickie would blow it, and Terry would quit what he was doing and race home to keep from getting into trouble. He would arrive at his back door only to be told by his mother that she hadn't whistled him home. Even after Dickie quit jerking Terry around, Terry assumed the whistle he had just heard wasn't his mother's and he ignored it. Mr. or Mrs. Weeks would then come find him and drag him home, scolding him the entire way.

The Cole boys enjoyed fooling around. Charlie Pace lived next door to them on their North side. Charlie was an only child and he was accorded lots of attention from his parents. One Sunday morning, Charlie came outside and was killing time waiting for his mom and dad to come get in the car so they could all go to church. Mrs. Pace had dressed Charlie to the nines in shorts, a bow tie and a sports jacket—not the way most of us in our neighborhood dressed. Dickie and John Cole saw Charlie all duded up and decided to have some fun at his expense. They crept around their house, turned on the water hose and drenched Charlie before he knew what hit him. Now, make no mistake about it, Charlie wasn't a sissy. However, I do believe that was the last day Charlie ever wore shorts—at least around the Cole boys.

The optimism and good feelings that pervaded post-war America, the freedom to roam our neighborhoods without suppressive supervision or fear of druggies or perverts, being forced outside by the lack of air conditioning in our homes, a scarcity of television sets and no electronic games or cell phones fueled the imaginations of us kids of the '50s. We were allowed to seek adventure and we did. From morning until dusk, we roamed around testing our wings. We learned to embrace victories and shake off defeats. We weren't particularly coddled. We were applauded when we did something good. We were punished when we did something bad. We didn't expect a trophy if we lost. Our parents were our parents, not our best buddies. They set the rules, and we followed them—or else. They defined our roles, and they let us be kids. It was a great time to be a kid.

Chapter 7
Trikes, Bikes, and a 1956 Pontiac

When you are too small and too young to drive a car, you need a two-wheeler. When you are too small for a two-wheeler, you need a three-wheeler. From 1949–1952, I raced around Marshall's Southside on a red and white trike, or tricycle for those of you with a bent toward formality. While some of the kids had trikes with fender skirts and multi-colored plastic tassels that dangled from their handlebar grips, mine didn't. It was a stripped-down trike. When I complained to Daddy about the lack of accessories on my trike, he told me the addition of those kinds of things just slowed down a trike, and that mine was a racing model. I bought his story. It never dawned on me that my trike just cost less than the fancier models. Besides, Daddy was proven right many times, because my "racer" never lost a trike race down Barrett's Hill.

Every now and then, the older boys of the neighborhood would get bored, round up all of us little guys, and have us bring our trikes to the corner of Nathan Street and Bomar Street. They would line us up facing south on Bomar. They would pat us on the back, verbally charge us up and whip us into a state of frenzy about the importance of the race that was about to happen. By the time they hollered "Go!" I was pretty near hyperventilating. I now wonder if they had bets on the race. The race length was one driveway short of one block long. The course was slightly downhill, full of trike-wrecking potholes and ended with a sharp left turn into the Barrett's driveway. That's why we dubbed it "Barrett's Hill." I really liked those races, probably because I won most of them. I put a lot of tough miles on my trike, and by the time I had to move up to my first bicycle, it was as worn out as the knees on my Roebuck jeans. At that point in my life, I had bonded with my trike and truly hated to transition from it to my next transportation phase.

The Christmas before I started first grade, Santa brought me my first bike. Like my trike, it was red and white and had no frills attached to it—not even a kick stand. Obviously, it—like my trike had been before it—was a racing model. All my buddies with whom I would be starting first grade got bikes that Christmas, too. Receiving them at Christmas gave us time to learn how to ride them well enough to enable us to ride them to school when September rolled around.

Terry got a beautiful maroon Schwinn with a headlight, a horn, a silver chain guard and some more of those tassels that dangled from his white handlebar grips. Charlie got a decked-out, black pee-wee bike with hand brakes that reeked of cool. David Reeves got a top-of-the-line bike like they sold at Western Auto. All their bikes had kick-stands, too. Their bikes were all small enough for them to be able to get on and off with relative ease. They could even reach the pedals without encountering the steel bar that ran from the seat to the handlebars. My new wheels were made by J. C. Higgins and measured twenty-four inches tall. It was clearly the biggest bike in the new crop of two-wheelers in our neighborhood. Truthfully, it was just too big for me.

The only way I could mount my bike was to get a running start and jump in the direction of the seat. I had to land just right on the seat or a crash was going to happen. More than once, my effort at mounting my bike ended up in a testicular disaster. If I landed well and managed to gain control of the bike, I then had to place my sneakers on the spinning pedals to be able to keep my speed up enough to avoid the bike's running out of steam and falling over. I had to engage the pedals when they were in the top of their rotations because my legs weren't long enough to reach the pedals when they were in the lower half of their rotations. This leg-length deficiency was a real problem. It meant I couldn't put on the brakes when it came time to stop. Take it from me, a man on a bike with no brakes is a man out of control. As I was trying to learn how to deal with my "short"-comings, I rode by my daddy as he was watering our camellias and yelled that I couldn't stop. He calmly advised me to seek out a soft-landing spot—but to not even consider using any of his prized camellias to break my fall. I think I had just received an early lesson in coping. As I circled the yard in search of a relatively safe place for dismounting, I decided I only had two choices: the cedar bush or the holly bush. Even to a six-year-old, that was an "oh hell" moment. At first, the cedar bush seemed like the better of the two choices. However, Daddy kept it severely pruned, and any one of the stubbed-off branches could have impaled me through the heart. Also, I knew there was at least one wasp nest in the cedar bush. On the other hand, the leaves of the holly bush were covered with needle-like spines that would show no mercy to a kid who jumped into the middle of them. I opted for the holly bush, rode alongside it, and bailed into the center of it, letting the bike coast on to a mild crash. Daddy walked over and helped me disentangle myself from the fully-armed holly bush. I was whimpering like a scared puppy, and I looked like I had been dragged through a briar patch by a runaway mule. Daddy rinsed off some of the scratches and poke-holes with the hose, looked me over, and pronounced me fit and able. He walked away with a slight smile on his face. I guess he viewed my bike-bush wreck as a learning experience. He was always big on us three boys having "learning experiences." He was from the old school, the one that thought suffering a little pain would toughen you up. I can't say this episode toughened me up, but I can assure you it scratched me up.

I still couldn't reach the brakes by the time school started. It was a good ten to twelve blocks from my house to South Marshall Elementary School, and I had to cross South Washington Street, which was a major street with lots of traffic. My bike had no basket, and backpacks (a.k.a. book bags) had not yet been discovered. Therefore, I had to carry my school supplies and books while trying to get on or off my big bike. That was a very tough assignment for a very small boy. The first day of biking to school presented me with two additional major challenges. First, how was I going to get across Washington Street? Second, how was I going to stop my bike once I got to school? I solved the getting-across-Washington problem by diving into a big gardenia bush in the yard of the last house before the intersection of Nathan and South Washington. After my many, many run-ins with the holly bush, it was almost fun to "hit" the gardenia bush. I then recouped my bike and gear and walked it across South Washington when there was no traffic. There were no gardenia bushes at the school, just a hard-packed clay schoolyard liberally strewn with sandstone rocks. It also had one of those long, metal bike racks with slots for the front tires. Crashing on the school ground in front of all those kids would have been terribly embarrassing, so I chose to use the bike rack. After doing reconnaissance on it during a couple of ride-bys, I developed a plan. I would coast up to the rack so that when

I reached it, I would be barely rolling. I would then aim my front tire for the slot and "ease" into it, allowing the rack to put the final stop on my bike. It all went pretty much according to plan, except that I was still going a little fast when I "slotted" my front tire. When my handlebar hit the top rail of the bike rack, the bike stopped, but I didn't. I smushed (much worse than smashed) my pecker and testicles on the bike's handlebar joint and proceeded to fly over the top of the rack, ultimately landing at the foot of some of my new classmates in a cloud of dust. My first order of business was to uncross my eyes, which was caused by the trauma to my privates. Having done a fairly good job at that, I gathered my strewn school supplies and tried to convince them I had done it all on purpose. I think Esta Zoe Cowan and Amanda Stallcup were the only ones who believed me. It was a devastating experience in more ways than one.

My inglorious bike stoppages went on teetering between disaster and mildly injurious until late November, at which time I discovered I had grown enough to be able to use the brakes. During the eleven months of "bush landings" I had endured, I got to know tons about the bushes and soft grass spots in our neighborhood. I've had lots of yards in my life, but I have never allowed a cedar or a holly bush to sink its roots into my dirt—not once.

I was running late for school one morning while in the sixth grade and asked Daddy to drive me so I wouldn't be tardy. Apparently, Daddy wasn't in the mood for the

eleven-block ride to South Marshall Elementary that morning
so he tossed me the keys to our 1956 Pontiac and told me to
drive carefully. As a twelve-year-old, I had only driven the
car a couple of times, and that had been under the careful and
critical eye of Daddy. The last time I had driven with Daddy, I
hit a serious pothole that rattled our bones. In response, Daddy
told me to stop the car and back it up about a hundred yards.
He then pointed at another pothole and told me to drive into
it, informing me that it was the only one I had missed the
entire drive. Point made, point taken. Daddy had an unusual
but effective teaching style. But back to the story about driving to school. When I realized that Daddy was serious about
me taking the car to school, I slipped behind the steering
wheel—which I could barely see over—cranked-up the big
V-8, and started trying to back out of our driveway. Daddy
stood by and successfully coached me into the street. He then
waved good-bye, turned around, and walked back inside.

As I eased the Pontiac toward school, I didn't know
whether to scream with joy, pee in my pants, or pull over and
vomit. When South Marshall came into view, my anxieties
turned into sheer pride. I couldn't wait for my classmates to
see me drive up. I knew how Lindberg felt when he landed in
Paris, and I couldn't wait to wallow in the wave of adoration
that was sure to greet my arrival. Unfortunately, by the time
I made it to school, everyone was already inside. My grand
entrance went unnoticed. Drat. I did experience an "I'm hot
shit moment" at recess when all my friends saw the car and

learned of my great adventure. One person who wasn't too impressed with my maiden solo flight was our principal who called my dad to inform him that I had obviously "stolen" our car and brought it to school. Daddy thanked him for his concern but assured him I had his permission to drive it to school. End of discussion. After school, I drove straight home. Daddy didn't make a big deal of it all, so I thought this might have been the first of many times I would be allowed to drive to school. Wrong. It never happened again, thanks, in large part, to the hissy-fit Mother threw when she found out what Daddy had done. Even today, I hold green and white 1956 Pontiacs in high esteem.

My trikes, bikes and our 1956 Pontiac allowed me to expand my world. There were many days when I couldn't figure out what I wanted to do, so I would hop on my trike or bike and take off for the unknown. I always found a new adventure.

One of the favorite things for my friends and me to do was to roar through the neighborhood with baseball cards fastened to our bikes in such a way that the cards struck the spokes on our wheels as they rolled. The cards were held in place by clothes pins, and the resultant clattering made our bikes sound like motorcycles—at least in our minds. Since I was an avid baseball card collector, I was very careful as to which players' cards I used for this purpose. I would never use a Mantle, Mays, Aaron or Snider card. Instead, I used cards of players like Wally Westlake, Lou Berberet, Bill Renna, Willie

Miranda and Jim Delsing. You see, once you used a card on your bike, the process bent the dickens out of it and it was no longer a worthy member of your highly valued collection. Even so, I always hated to sacrifice a baseball card just to get to ride along with our version of Hell's Angels.

My mother, Zelma, was an avid bridge player, and she played every Tuesday night with Liz Galik, Leola Reynolds and Zelda Waghalder for more than forty years. Liz, Leola, Zelda and Zelma were quite a foursome, and the things I remember most about their bridge games were that they all talked at the same time and that Zelda was the partner they all least wanted. They loved Zelda, but she apparently was seldom on top of her game. She and Leola were older than Liz and Mother, and I remember they both wore their hose rolled down to below their knees. It must have been more comfortable to wear hose that way, but it sure didn't make much of a fashion statement. Yuck! Mother's love of bridge fits into this chapter about bikes and trikes because one time I made the near-fatal mistake of clothes-pinning some of Mother's brand-new plastic playing cards to my bike instead of using my highly prized baseball cards. Plastic playing cards were new to the market and were quite expensive when compared to the cost of regular playing cards (which happened to be called "Bicycle Cards"). When I inspected the new cards, I noticed they were stiffer, yet more flexible, than baseball cards. In my *Eureka!* moment that followed, I decided they would make the perfect noisemakers for my bike. I pinned them on and rode off to show my technology breakthrough to Terry, Charlie and Clarence. They were duly impressed, so I got to lead the gang that day. After "terrorizing" the neighborhood for an hour or so, I went home, parked my "hog", and returned the cards to their double deck box. That Tuesday night, Mother hosted the "girls." She meticulously placed the table in the center of the living room, put coasters in just the right places, made sure the score-keeping pencil was sharp and proudly laid out her new plastic cards. After going gaga over the new cards and exchanging pleasantries, they got down to business. Leola dealt. After the four of them picked-up their cards and fanned them before their eyes, a curious pall settled in. It seems that some of the cards had no numbers or suits on them. Of course, the numberless cards were the ones I had clipped on my bike the afternoon before. It didn't take Mother long to nail yours truly for the crime I had committed. Mother confined me to my small bedroom and told me she "would deal with me later." She did. It seems that while the "new" cards were made to stand up to the spokes without breaking or permanently bending, their numbers and suits that had been printed on them flaked off when struck by several thousand encounters with spinning spokes. I returned to using baseball cards. It was safer.

The Christmas of my fifth grade, I got a new twenty-six-inch deluxe bike by J. C. Higgins. It had a horn, kick stand, cool handlebar grips and a jazzed-up chain guard. It was red and white and drop-dead gorgeous. I was in "high cotton" when I rode this beauty, and, thank God, I could reach the pedals with ease. My transportation euphoria lasted only a couple of months, though, because one morning as I was riding to school, I hit a pothole and my new, super-duper bike broke in half. It didn't crack or bend; it broke in half. With a heavy heart, I pulled the two halves out of the street, left them in a grassy spot next to the Lanier's driveway, and walked on to school. After school, I retrieved my bike—which now was truly a "bi"-cycle—and piled it in our front yard. I don't know if warranties were different back then, but I do know that bike was never replaced. Maybe Daddy thought asking Sears for a replacement would have been like begging. I don't

I was so proud of my new, fancy J.C. Higgins bike. It broke in two after two months and was never replaced.

know. But Daddy was like that. Thank goodness I still had my trusty old bike.

My trikes and bikes allowed me to expand my world. There were many days when I couldn't figure out what I wanted to do, so I would hop on my trike or bike and take off for the unknown. I always found a new adventure. My trikes and bikes were important to me, and, as an adult, when I dig deeply into my memory bank, I can still feel the seats and handlebar grips of those much-loved vehicles. The senses of discovery and excitement I felt all those years ago are rekindled in me. Even faint romantic memories of JoAnn Efurd and Ruth Ann McClaran race through my mind. Yep, I rode them into many, many good times.

Chapter 8
Chief Ezell and Miss Roma

Our house was on the corner of Grove Street and Medill Street. It faced east, and it fronted on Grove. The Ezell's house was also on the corner of Grove and Medill. It faced south and fronted on Medill. Their house faced the side of our house. Suffice it to say, the Ezells were our neighbors. They were good neighbors, and they sort of "adopted" me as their own. In fact, Mizz Ezell kept a running measurement of my height from age four up until I was fifteen. She kept it next to the door that led into her kitchen from their garage. Their one son, Clarence Jr., was grown, gone and childless, so I guess I was like a grandson to them. Clarence Jr. and his wife Nita were also very attentive and loving to me and included me in lots of their activities. The entire Ezell Family was like a second family to me. The thing I most remember about Clarence Jr. was that he had the biggest Adam's apple

I had ever seen, and when he chuckled, it bobbed vigorously up and down.

Mr. Ezell was our city's long-serving chief of police, and everyone in town just called him "Chief." Before becoming our chief, he had been an officer in the Texas Highway Patrol and a member of the Texas Rangers. While he was serving in one of those highly-respected organizations, Chief became the first motorcycle patrolman in Texas, which made him a minor legend in East Texas. By the time I was old enough to remember Chief, he was nearing retirement. He was sort of frail and slow moving, but he was still in charge and proved to be a man of action.

It was pretty common in the 1950s for an outbreak of rabies to sweep through town. Back then, lots of folks didn't bother getting their pets vaccinated against rabies and most dogs were "outdoors" dogs free to roam, so when a rabid dog was spotted, the whole town went on alert. Everyone was advised to tie up their dogs or put them in pens until the situation was well in hand. Typically, a "mad dog" would wander aimlessly through the streets. It would do so at a fast walking pace. It would stare straight ahead, and it often foamed at the mouth. Non-infected dogs would see the strange dog pass through their territory and attack it to protect their turf. The rabid dog would fight with super strength and a single mindedness that enabled it to win most all its battles. It also usually bit its attacker during the scrape, thus infecting the other dog with the deadly virus. That fight cycle repeated itself over and over, ultimately creating a rabies epidemic and all the fright that went with it. When rabies hit town, the neighborhoods became as quiet as crowded elevators because parents wouldn't let their kids play outside without parental supervision, and all the dogs were either tied up or in pens.

Late one summer afternoon, Terry and I were playing in my yard when our hound, Belle, started howling and tore out after a black mixed breed that was speed walking on Grove Street in front of our house. Belle tried to attack the intruder, but it simply snapped at her, shoved her to the side, and continued on its trek to who-knows-where. Belle was unhurt, but Terry and I noticed she had foamy dog spit all over her back. We watched the dog continue its travels south on Grove. It looked and acted "mad" to us, so we ran to Chief's house to report our suspicions. Chief and Mrs. Ezell were sitting in their backyard enjoying cold drinks. When we told them our tale, chief went in his house and came out with his big, nickel-plated revolver. He put us in his police car and off we went in search of the dog in question. We spotted it about five blocks from our house, and chief told us he thought we were right about it being mad. The dog was walking through backyards that ran up to the edge of Grove Street. Chief held his pistol in his right hand, leaned it across his left forearm and started firing at the dog. We were rolling along Grove at a pace equal to the dog's gait. Chief was holding the steering wheel with his left hand, and he kept switching his vision from the road to the dog,

85

the dog to the road, and so on. He wasn't shooting or driving very well because we kept running off the road, and he kept missing the dog with his errant shots. Chief was really old and darned-near blind at that time. His glasses were slabs of glass, and, I guess, they should have been even thicker, because his bullets were throwing up dirt all around the mad dog but did nothing to cause the dog to alter its course. Terry and I looked at each other and silently shared the knowledge that we were seeing an epic saga unfold right before our very eyes. We both wondered about the wisdom of firing real bullets toward the houses, but, obviously, Chief wasn't concerned because he kept firing. Finally, one of his bullets found its mark and the dog went down. Chief stopped the car, reloaded, walked over to the writhing dog and put a slug through its head. He then took a shovel out of the trunk of his '57 Ford, scooped up the dog, and put it in the trunk. After he dropped Terry and me off, he drove off to where chiefs of police go when they have a dead rabid dog in their trunk.

Daddy took Belle to our local vet, Dr. Joe Black, for an inspection. He washed her down good, looked her over closely and determined she was good-to-go since her skin had not been broken. We later learned the dog Chief killed was indeed rabid. It must not have bitten any other dogs, because there were no more reported cases of the fierce disease. Terry and I became neighborhood heroes to our peers for a week or so because of our adventure with Chief. As I think back on that incident, I can't give Chief high praise for marksmanship or for having the good sense to not sling lead all over our neighborhood from a moving vehicle, but I can unabashedly proclaim him as a man of action.

Mrs. Roma Ezell, or Mizz Ezell as I called her, raised and sold parakeets. She had a large, screened-in shed in her backyard just boiling over with the fidgety, brightly colored little birds. It was screened from floor to roof on all four sides. On slow days in the neighborhood, I would often go sit in the shade by the bird house and just watch the little blurs of blue, white and yellow flit around from roost to roost. I was the only kid in the neighborhood who had a "pass" to do so. When Mizz Ezell spotted me bird watching, she nearly always brought me a welcomed glass of lemonade or ice water. I was often joined in admiring the parakeets by one or more salivating cats. They lurked under the cherry laurel trees near the back of the shed. You could tell they were tortured to their toes by being so close to all those tasty critters, yet unable to "enjoy" their company. I could kind of empathize with the cats, because I felt the same way when I looked in the window at the local bakery and didn't have a penny to my name. The cats made the birds super nervous, so when they came around, Mizz Ezell would chase them away by swatting at them with her broom.

Even though Marshall passed a law making it illegal to shoot BB guns inside the city limits when I was about nine or ten, Chief gave me full cat-shootin' privileges so long as

I didn't shoot toward the birds. I wasn't popular with the local cats, but I was the envy of all of my BB gun-owning friends. It was lucky for the cats that my J. C. Higgins BB gun from Sears, Roebuck & Company had very little power. Even if I scored a direct hit with it, it might sting the cat a bit, but darn sure didn't hurt it. Terry had a high-powered, pump BB gun that would have put a hurtin' on a cat. It was lucky for the cats Terry didn't have hunting privileges in the Ezell's backyard.

Mizz Ezell had a pet parakeet that was well known throughout Marshall. His name was Chuckie, and he had a better vocabulary that most of the citizens of our fair city. Chuckie was bright yellow and totally remarkable. He not only could talk, but he also could recognize people and would call them by name. Anytime I walked up their front or rear steps, Chuckie would announce me by saying, "Scotty's here! Scotty's here!" When the postman would bring the mail up the steps, Chuckie would tell Mizz Ezell, "The mail's here!" Chuckie achieved stardom after the daily newspaper ran a full-page story about the avian orator, complete with pictures. Teachers would sometimes bring their classes to the Ezell's house to see Chuckie perform, and, one time, an enterprising radio newsman actually interviewed Chuckie on live radio. Stage fright wasn't in Chuckie's make up, so his interview went off without a snag. He didn't just talk; he talked well. His enunciation was top drawer. The only problem was that Chuckie never shut up. The only way to get him quiet was to put him in his cage, cover it and move it to the back bedroom.

Mizz Ezell gave me a blue and white parakeet which, for some reason, I named Billy. My entire family tried to teach Billy to talk, but all Billy ever said was, "My name is Billy." My brother, Robert, tried to teach Billy to say, "I smell shit." Billy was either too dumb to learn it, or too smart to say it. I never really bonded with Billy, because I never figured out what one did with a bird to have fun. I still don't know. I do know I got tired of cleaning Billy's cage.

The day Chuckie died was a sad day in the neighborhood. Mizz Ezell was inconsolable for weeks, and I missed the little fellow, too. The Ezells wrapped Chuckie in silk, put him in a cigar box, sealed it with wax and buried him under a cherry laurel tree in their backyard. Mizz Ezell, Chief and I were the only ones at the funeral.

Chief retired when I was about twelve or thirteen, and Mizz Ezell quit raising parakeets about the same time. During this wind-down phase of their lives, they turned their attention to yard work, fishing and late afternoon cocktails under the shade tree in their backyard. Their yard was pretty, they caught lots of fish, and they DID enjoy their cocktails.

They did most of their fishing at Harris Lake. It was a privately owned lake and very few folks were granted fishing privileges there. I guess Chief still had some pull, because he and Mizz Ezell could fish the fifteen-to-twenty-acre lake at will. When I said they caught lots of fish, I wasn't joking.

They pole-fished for bream and often caught eighty to a hundred of the little perches. They kept everything they caught, regardless of how puny they were. They must have realized Mother and Daddy had their hands full trying to keep three growing boys full, so they got to where they would bring most of their catch to our house. The fish were uncleaned, and, for the most part, no bigger than the palm of a petite lady's left hand. Daddy quickly figured out that gutting and scaling those scrawny, bony little critters was time poorly spent considering the ultimate payoff. However, not wanting to hurt the Ezell's feelings, Daddy would thank them profusely and accept their alms. He would then wait until dark, and bury them around the bases of our eight or so fruit trees in the backyard. We were coached on how to profess our gratitude to Chief and Mizz Ezell for the fish and how to tell them how much we enjoyed them.

I can tell you for sure that fish make a wonderful fertilizer for fruit trees, because ours were the healthiest looking pear and peach trees in all of Marshall. Their leaves were a dark, rich green and the fruit they produced was huge and reputedly delicious. I say "reputedly" because I seldom ate any of our homegrown fruit. I preferred to steal my pears from the Pace's tree, because I was convinced I could taste fish when I ate our pears. Daddy told me I was just being stupid, but I handled that moniker with ease. If I was so stupid, why did cats repeatedly walk circles around our fruit trees?

My two brothers, Homer and Robert, were thirteen and ten years older than me. I was four or five at this time. They were both away at college by the time I was nine. I missed them terribly, so I would get hyperexcited when they would come home for the weekend or for holidays. When they came home, lots of their friends would come to our house and everyone would sit around telling stories and laughing. Often, Jack Seaburn and Wayne Scoggins showed up with their guitars and a gospel songfest would break out. My brothers had excellent voices so they often sang duets while everyone else kept time by tapping their toes or slapping their thighs. They were quite often joined by their girlfriends, Freddie and Nancy, both of whom also had good singing voices and made it a super quartet. They would also let me sing with them when they sang "When the Saints Go Marching In" and "Do Lord." I thought I was really good, but now I realize my brothers were the stars. Inevitably, several folks would bring alcoholic beverages, which were quickly declared community property, and before long the house was jumping with songs like "Down by the Riverside," "Swing Low Sweet Chariot," "Amazing Grace," "Precious Memories" and "Let That Circle Be Unbroken." Jack Seaburn was a fine guitarist, but he couldn't hold his booze. He had the unusual ability to pass out right in the middle of a strum on his Gibson. He would stay in that state of frozen guitar pickin' until the session ended sometime after midnight.

Another character who usually showed up at our gospel nights was one of Daddy's American Legion drinking buddies named Bish Little. Bish and his twin brother Buck were from the little town of Elysian Fields, which was ten or twelve miles from Marshall. Buck was a deputy sheriff and Bish was an "unofficial" deputy sheriff. The twins were well known throughout the county for being tough as boots and twice as nasty. Reputedly, Bish carried a straight-edged razor in his khakis and was quick to use it. I later found out he actually kept the razor in a scabbard he had had sewn inside his boot. The music and the whiskey always mellowed Bish right out, and he sang along with everyone. However, his favorite song was "Precious Memories," and he always got to perform a solo when it was played. He would stand, sweep the room with his rheumy eyes and go to singing. His singing rated about a C, but his sincerity rated a solid A+. Without fail, when the line ". . . precious memories, how they linger" was due to be sung, Bish would sing ". . . precious memories, how they *lingo*." No one ever asked him why he said "lingo" instead of "linger." I guess it just didn't matter much. Bish infused wherever he was with a richness of character. He was different from most folks and I was always proud he felt at home with our family. Daddy used to tell us boys how tough Bish was, and Bish would tell us how tough Daddy was. I suspect they were both right.

Since we had no air conditioning in our little house, all our windows were open throughout the night. The music that flowed through those windows was tolerated by most of our neighbors, but it lured some of the less timid of them over to our house so they could be part of the fun. In truth, it was darned good music, too, and that caused quite a few folks to drop in. Chief and Mizz Ezell always came over and took part in the festivities. The more Mizz Ezell drank, the more she sang. Singing wasn't her strong suit, but volume was. Daddy once said she had been around parakeets so long, she sounded like them. When the party was over, we'd wake Chief up and Homer or Robert would walk him and Mizz Ezell home. I should also mention that our next-door neighbor, Zel Oller, a local cobbler, often brought his guitar over and played along with Jack and Wayne. He played an old Stella guitar and he could flat tear it up. At the end of the evening, several of my brothers' friends would sleep on our living room floor. Bish usually got the sofa. The next morning, Mother and Daddy would cook breakfast for us and our extended family and then send them on their way.

We moved from South Grove Street when I was fifteen. Chief and Mizz Ezell were quite old by then and had become pretty frail. Like most of us when we get old, the Ezells got to where they talked mostly about their failing health—particularly Mizz Ezell. Daddy had to quit working in the side yard that faced the Ezell's house because when he did, Mizz Ezell would spot him and come over and bend his ear for an hour or so about her various ailments. Daddy came in the house one afternoon from weeding in the side yard and collapsed in our big green chair. Mother told him he looked pale and asked him if he was okay. Daddy looked up at her and replied, "Hell no, I'm not okay. I just spent one hour and twenty minutes hearing in great detail about Roma's collapsed rectum." From then on, Daddy crept around our yard like a cat burglar casing a house.

The Ezells lived until I was in my twenties. I would stop by for visits with them occasionally. I could always count on a hug and a glass of either lemonade or ice water. They were special to me. They shared their love with me, and I returned it freely to them.

Chapter 9
Mr. Eddie's Fence

Maybe growing up in Marshall when I did was like growing up in most places at that time. I don't know. I can only talk about Marshall, and more specifically, the Southside of Marshall. That was my world, and I liked it.

It was a time and place where everybody knew each other; there were very few secrets, even fewer air conditioners and most folks didn't lock their doors. Kids and dogs ran free, shoes were optional in the summer and, if you wore them, it was because you had stickers in your yard. Bicycles had no gears and there were no fences in the neighborhood—except one. Eddie Hynson had a fence.

Eddie—Mr. Hynson to us kids—lived behind us on about an acre with his wife and four daughters: Joyce, Rosalee, Dud and Dooley. Mr. Eddie was a house painter and carpenter when he wasn't running trotlines for catfish at Caddo Lake. He had built their small house all by himself. It had two stories, with the downstairs being nothing but a storage area and small workshop. The second story provided modest living quarters for the family of six. Their house was one of the few in the neighborhood that wasn't hooked up to city water and sewer. They had their own well and they washed their clothes in a big, black, iron pot set on an open fire behind the house. Their septic tank was also behind their house, and Eddie must not have been big on cleaning it because it was in a constant mushy state that wasn't sensory-pleasing. The house was well-kept and kind of neat, with a cool front yard shaded by some massive oaks.

When Mr. Eddie built his house, he put it toward the front of his acre leaving most of his remaining three-fourths of an acre for use as a large garden. The entire Hynson Family worked in the garden and they successfully grew peas, beans, onions, turnip greens, radishes and corn. They probably grew other stuff, too, but those are the ones I remember. Most of the men in the neighborhood envied Eddie's garden, perhaps because most of them had grown up on farms.

Each spring, Mr. Eddie—dressed in his ever-present denim overalls and often shirtless under them—hooked his mule up to his plow and carved his plot into neat rows, making it ready for planting. Mr. Eddie and his mule were cut from the same cloth. Both were large, big-footed, swaybacked, potbellied plodders that went about their business as though they were walking through quicksand and being paid by the hour. The mule must have been rented, because it was only around for about a week or two when Mr. Eddie was putting his garden in and about the same amount of time when the garden was spent and Eddie turned his soil over so it could recharge for next spring's planting. When the mule was in residence, Mr. Eddie rigged a make-do, barbed wire fence behind his house to keep the mule from roaming South Marshall. It wasn't much of a fence, but it was the only one in my stomping grounds. Mr. Eddie used the back wall of his house for part of the fence and incorporated a small wooden shed within its borders. It became a somewhat memorable fence over time, and here's why.

As I said, Mr. Eddie split his time between painting houses and fishing for catfish. No matter which of the two he was doing on a given day, he quite often managed to find time to get a tad tipsy on moonshine—yes, real moonshine, which was commonplace in rural East Texas. The more Mr. Eddie drank, the fouler his mood became and the louder he got. Sometimes, late into the evening, he would go on a rampage before hitting the sack. A rampage by Mr. Eddie meant show time for the whole neighborhood. Since we didn't have air conditioners, everyone slept with their windows open, so when Mr. Eddie started his thunderous bellowing of profanities, EVERYONE in the neighborhood heard it all. Not only did Mr. Eddie cuss and holler, he often grabbed his double-barreled shotgun and fired it indiscriminately out his upstairs window. That was bad enough, but it got worse. When the shotgun blasts went off, the old mule, whose pen was right beneath the window, would wake up and decide it was time to get the hell out of Hynsonville. He would jump the fence and go ripping through the neighborhood. Mr. Eddie would yell something akin to "that damned old mule done jumped the fence and flew the coop!" With that pronouncement, the men of the neighborhood knew it was round-up time. They hastily threw on some clothes, went outside and dispersed throughout the neighborhood as though being deployed by Patton. The mission: find Mr. Eddie's mule and return it to him. It was a scene that repeated itself two or three times a year. It was a pain in the ass for the men, but it was just something that had to be done. By the time the men returned the mule, Mr. Eddie seemed to have been sobered up enough by the incident to feel some remorse and say "thank you" to the round-up crew. Nobody—with the probable exception of Mrs. Hynson and their girls—got angry with Mr. Eddie. That was just Mr. Eddie, and he was part of the package that was my neighborhood, which was filled with plenty of folks with demons of their own to battle.

To support that last statement, let me tell you about what happened one night in our neighborhood involving a neighbor named Bill. Bill had come home from the war with the ghosts of battle still racing around in his head. He turned to alcohol for relief and became an alcohol abuser. Late one evening, we heard noises coming from our garage. Daddy and Homer were elected to check it out. When they did, they found Bill huddled in the back corner of our garage. Daddy and Homer escorted him into the house and tried to calm him. He was in his pajamas and his knees were bleeding profusely. It was obvious he had been running and had fallen, skinning his knees mercilessly. Daddy got Bill to lay down on our sofa, and Mother cleaned and doctored his knees. Bill wasn't making much sense and kept ranting about someone trying to kill him. His eyes were huge and darted rapidly from one person to another. His fear was carved on his pale face. Daddy thought Bill was suffering from delirium tremens and sat beside him all night. When Daddy called Bill's wife the next morning to let her know he was okay and where he was, he found out that she had been chasing Bill with a butcher knife the night before in hopes of killing him. Bill was right. The couple divorced and his wife was never charged. Bill went through A.A. and stayed sober the remaining years of his life. Neither he nor his ex-wife ever remarried. Can you blame them? As I said, a whole lot of demons lived behind the walls of the neat little houses of our neighborhood.

Back to Mr. Eddie. I can't talk about him without telling about a memorable event in our neighborhood that involved him. Late one afternoon, I was playing with Charlie at his house, which was next door to the Hynson's, when Mr. Eddie pulled his black 1939 Chevy pickup truck into his dirt driveway and parked under one of his huge oaks. When he got out of his truck, he hollered for Charlie and me to come see what he had. We were always a little afraid of Mr. Eddie because of his size and gruff voice, but our curiosity got the best of us and we went over to his truck. He then pulled a tarpaulin off of something and lowered his tailgate. When he lowered the tailgate, a giant fish tail flopped down and actually touched the ground. What Charlie and I saw in that truck stunned us to silence. We were in a state of total disbelief. It was the biggest catfish we had ever seen. It weighed 125 pounds and Mr. Eddie had caught it on one of his trot lines at Caddo Lake. It was longer than his truck bed and spilled out of the back onto the dirt. I don't know how they found out, but, before long, quite a few neighborhood folks had gathered around Eddie's truck just gawking at the fish in amazement. Someone called the *Marshall News Messenger*, our local daily newspaper, and told them about Mr. Eddie's catch. They quickly dispatched a photographer to record Eddie's ascension into East Texas angling lore. It was a special day, and I still remember the humble look of pride on Mr. Eddie's face as all his neighbors patted him on the back and gushed over his accomplishment. I also remember seeing his family relishing in Mr. Eddie's glory. Good for Mr. Eddie. He deserved a break.

The Hynsons had a corn crib where they stored all the ears of unhusked corn their garden produced. Terry, Charlie and I had heard corn silk was good to smoke. Since we were into trying new things, we decided to raid Mr. Eddie's corn crib and harvest a load of corn silk. While we were partially husking his corn in search of the golden silk, Mr. Eddie stopped by and asked us what we were doing. Too frightened to lie, we told him the truth. Our fear of being beaten half to death was uncalled for, as he simply told us not to start any fires

(L to R) Scotty, Terry and Charlie playing on Terry's swing set. Looks like Terry is about to perform some daring-do on the trapeze. I think he was faking.

and to be watchful for the rats that had invaded his crib. He was smart, because the rat rumor caused us to hastily retreat from his corn crib. We had enough corn silk to experiment with smoking it, but we must have done something wrong. All we did was to burn our fingers and our lips.

As an aside, it should be noted that folks didn't look down their noses at Mr. Eddie or his family. We all had family members and friends on water wells and septic systems. We all had family members and friends with drinking problems. No one in our neighborhood had any money. As a matter of fact, the Hynsons were no different from any of us. Mrs. Hynson was a very highly-respected nurse in Marshall. Joyce, the oldest of the girls, who was a pretty blonde, married well and moved away. Rosalee was the daughter who looked and walked most like her daddy. She was always in a good mood and had the biggest boobs of all the sisters. All the older neighborhood boys used to love to watch her run and the resultant flopping action. She married young, had a bunch of kids and followed her mother into nursing. Dud was smart, good-looking and popular. She moved away and I lost track of her. Dooley, whose real name was Bernice, was as sweet a girl as ever drew a breath. She played in the band and was well-liked by all. Went on to graduate from college.

Mr. Eddie? Well, he died younger than he should have, but God knows he deserved the peace. One of a kind, Mr. Eddie. He will be remembered for a lot of things, but building a quality fence and holding his liquor aren't two of them.

Chapter 10
Smoking and Two Falstaffs

Daddy smoked. Both of my older brothers smoked. Aunts, uncles, cousins, family friends and coaches smoked. Our family doctor always had a Chesterfield hanging out of his mouth. Heck, even Ted Williams, Stan Musial and John Wayne smoked. President Eisenhower did, too. It was the 1950s and, as a small boy, it looked to me like smoking was the national pastime and something I needed to learn to do. Heck, they even made candy cigarettes so we could play like we were smoking. Parents didn't tell you smoking would kill you so don't do it. Their big threat was that it would stunt your growth—a tough sell to a kid who was noticeably taller than all his friends and had two older brothers well over six-foot tall. They just implored you to wait until you were older, like seventeen or eighteen. As an aside, I ended up being six feet, four inches tall. If I had waited until I was seventeen or eighteen to start smoking, I might have ended up six feet and eight inches or more. Who knows?

Because smoking was so popular, the opportunity to pilfer a cigarette from an open pack left lying around was ever present. "Pilfering" a cigarette sounds better than "stealing" a cigarette, but it was outright stealing. When you were only five or six years old and wanted to smoke, you had to steal a cigarette because you had no money to buy a pack and, besides, the adults who ran the neighborhood grocery stores wouldn't sell to a kid so young. You had to be at least twelve before they would take your quarter. Daddy smoked Camels, and since he was unknowingly my source for cigarettes, so did I. On the strength scale, Camels ranked #2, just behind Picayunes, which would cause a near-death experience with each drag.

My pre-school through about third grade smoking buddies were Terry Weeks and David Reeves. Smoking wasn't our obsession; playing war, cowboys and Indians, digging holes and getting dirty were top priorities. However, when the opportunity to smoke presented itself, we put down our guns, stick horses and shovels and went "smoking." There were lots of good hiding places for smoking in our neighborhood, but sometimes we didn't pick well.

David's dad was a candy distributor, and, in those days, candy distributors were also cigarette distributors. Mr. Reeves used his garage as his warehouse and one time David "found" a pack of Pall Malls so he shoved them in his pocket, hopped

on his trike and sought out Terry and me. We were at my
house playing cowboys. Terry was Roy Rogers and I was Lash
LaRue. When David flashed us his red pack of Pall Malls,
our attention immediately turned to finding a place to fire
up. We made a bad choice. We decided to take our adventure
to my closet. It was a very small closet and it was not just
my closet. It was the closet for both of my teenaged brothers
and me, and it was crammed full of our clothes and other
worldly goods. The fact that there was no wiggle room or
light in the closet didn't deter us. We closed ourselves in, lit
up and went to puff city. Our smoke output must have been
epic because Daddy, who was in the kitchen cooking a pot
of beans, smelled the smoke and walked into the bedroom
to investigate. He saw the smoke pouring through the gap
at the bottom of the door and quickly assumed something
in the closet was on fire. He yanked the door open only to
be engulfed by a giant, billowing cloud of gray smoke that
spilled out into the bedroom. After fighting through the fog,
Daddy found the three of us sitting on the closet floor staring up at him. He wasn't happy; not at all. After collecting
our burning cigarettes, he yanked me out of the closet and
spanked me in one swift motion. He promptly sent Terry and
David home with their tails tucked between their legs and
started fanning the smoke with a bath towel to usher it out
through an open window. The attic fan helped. I retreated
to the sofa in the living room where I tried to blend into the
green upholstery fabric.

I didn't achieve invisibility because Daddy walked over to me and stared down at me with a look of absolute incredulity on his face. While he was looming and staring, I figured out that his look expressed his surprise that I could be stupid enough to light up in a small, closed closet full of flammables. Message received. I inwardly gave a sigh of relief when the stare job and lecture stopped and Daddy returned to the kitchen. I was thinking I had weathered the storm, but it wasn't over. A couple of hours or so after the "bust," I was sitting on the living room floor playing with my toy soldiers when we heard a timid knock on our front door. Daddy answered the door with me standing behind him, peeping around his leg to see who it was. It was David. When Daddy asked what he wanted, David unflinchingly replied, "I left my cigarettes here and would like them back." Daddy retrieved the Pall Malls, gave them to David, and stood watching and shaking his head as David peddled off in search of his next adventure.

When I was about ten, another friend of mine, Johnny Galik, rode his bike to my house and suggested we hide in my garage and smoke the four L&Ms he had taken from his mother's unguarded pack. Johnny was two years older than me so I sort of looked up to him and followed his lead. This day, he proudly announced that he had learned how to blow smoke rings and that he would teach me how to do it, too. Turns out he not only could blow smoke rings, but he also could blow a large smoke ring and then send a smaller one through the big one. Johnny always was overloaded with talent. I did learn to blow smoke rings that day and I honed that skill for the next forty-five years. Johnny's mother Liz and my mother Zee (short for Zelma), along with Leola Reynolds and Zelda Waghalder, played bridge together every Tuesday night for more than forty years. Leola and Zelda were childless, so Liz and Mother hosted the game on an alternating basis to avoid babysitting problems. When Mother hosted, Johnny would accompany his mom to my house and we would play together. When the game was at the Galik's house down on Holland Street, I'd tag along so Johnny and I could play there. We usually played a lot of marbles, and even though we said we were playing "keepsies," Johnny usually gave me back the marbles he won off me. Johnny was just that way.

Elvis Presley got incredibly popular when I was in the sixth grade. Inspired by the King, long, greasy hair with duck-tails replaced crew cuts as the rage, and black leather or vinyl motorcycle jackets became a "must" for the hep cats. Terry and Tuck got real leather jackets, while most of my pals and me made do with the vinyl numbers. It was cool to look "thuggy." Andrew "Butch" Barton pulled off this new look better than all the rest of us. He really did look like a younger version of Elvis, right down to the sneer. These jackets had seven to ten separate zippered pockets. One pocket was reserved for your super-cool sunglasses, but it was a challenge to fill the other pockets with cool "stuff." My buds and I decided we all needed to carry a pack of smokes in one of our pockets. Because of the popularity of television's *The Mickey Mouse Club,* clubs of all sorts started popping up. Therefore, we took the next logical step and formed the South Marshall Smoking Club, kind of a bastardized merger of the Mickey Mouse Club and an Elvis fan club. At this point in the story, I should tell you that every boy in my age group in America had a deep and sincere crush on the Mouseketeer siren Annette Funicello.

Initially, we carried our cigarettes in our jackets, and after school we all headed to a nearby section of off-campus woods for a smoke. Our fear of being caught with our smokes on us led to each of us burying our cigarettes in an old tin can in the woods. Each day when school was out, we would meet in the woods, dig up our respective cans and conduct club business over a relaxing cigarette. The South Marshall Smoking Club had a short shelf life. Its failure could be attributed to any of five factors or a combination of those factors. First, there came a frog-strangling gully washer that dumped three or four inches of rain in our woods. After the storm, we dug up our smokes and discovered our cigarettes had turned to mush because our tin cans weren't waterproof. Second, Tuck was the only club member who had enough money to buy a pack of replacements for our soggy cigarettes. Third, some of the club members' parents got to wondering why their boys took so long to get home after school and imposed time limits on their walks or bike rides home from school. Fourth, our business meetings were boring because we had no business.

Fifth, baseball season was starting and we all played on little league teams and had practice after school.

When a new boy moved to our neighborhood, considerable time was spent sizing up the newcomer. Questions dealing with how tough he was, how fast he could run, how smart he was and how much fun you could have with him just had to be answered. Secretly, we also hoped he wouldn't be cool enough to steal our girlfriends. All the boys in the neighborhood sat around opining about whether the new kid would fit in. Such was the case when James Smith and his family moved to Marshall from somewhere in Mississippi. Since James, like me, was entering the sixth grade, I took it upon myself to check him out. He quickly made it known that his two favorite things to do were to pole vault and to smoke. He had just become the first pole vaulter in our neighborhood, but several us had him covered on the smoking bit.

The Smiths rented the white frame house behind Hartley's grocery store. It, like most of the houses in the neighborhood, was built on pier and beam, meaning you could crawl under it if you were in the mood for a dusty sanctuary. One afternoon, James scored a couple of Lucky Strikes from his dad's unattended pack and invited me to join him under his house for a smoke. All the while we were smoking, we could hear Mr. Smith's footfalls on the floor above our heads. What we didn't realize was that quite a few of the floor boards had separated in spots thus allowing our smoke from below to waft through the floor into the house where Mr. Smith could see it. Soon, we followed the sound of Mr. Smith's footsteps from the living room to the kitchen. We then heard the creaking sound of the back screen door being opened, followed by the clop, clop, clop of his big feet as they descended the back steps. By this time, James and I had frozen—afraid of what might be heading our way. Next, we could see Mr. Smith's legs from the knees down and they were heading our way. He then leaned over and yelled in our direction for us to get our asses out from under the house, pronto. Sheer panic and fear swallowed James whole. We quickly buried our cigarette butts, and, in desperation, James grabbed a handful of East Texas dust and ate it, hoping it would get the smell of nicotine off his breath and save him from a whoopin'. When we crawled out from under the house, we stood before Mr. Smith and he looked ten feet tall. He didn't seem to even notice me but he was staring a hole through James. In his haste, James had failed to wipe the excess dirt from his mouth and Mr. Smith was quick to figure out James's ploy aimed at avoiding punishment. In the wink of an eye, Mr. Smith grabbed James arm, spun him around and proceeded to wear out his guilty little butt. He then turned James's to face him, stared right into his eyes and said, "Boy, I'm not whipping you for smoking. I'm whipping you for being stupid enough to eat dirt!" I went home. But I went home having learned that it's often better to admit your guilt and take your punishment than it is to make hasty, poorly thought-out attempts at covering up your mistake.

During our smoking days, we often racked our brains to come up with a store that would sell us cigarettes. The Food Mart wouldn't. Hartley's wouldn't. Min-A-Pak wouldn't. It was frustrating to us wanna-be tough guys. Finally, we discovered Coleman's Store. Mr. Coleman, who was very old at the time, often had to be awakened when we entered his store in search of cigarettes. He was a super-nice old fellow who enjoyed our company and, of course, was amenable to selling us our cigarettes. He had some old lawn chairs in front of his tiny neighborhood store and we would all sit in them and talk for an hour or so with Mr. Coleman while he dipped snuff and we smoked. We boys developed a true friendship with Mr. Coleman, and we passed a lot of good times in his company.

In many respects, the freedom we had to roam our neighborhoods as kids led to us getting into more mischief than we would have in today's more closely-controlled environment. For example, Terry and I were playing in his garage one day when we discovered a six-pack of Falstaff beer hidden in a pile of scrap lumber. We knew it belonged to Terry's brother Gaines, who was about sixteen at the time. We were wizened ten-year olds and we opted to steal two cans for our own consumption. Terry found an opener in his daddy's tool chest. We took the beer and the opener to a spot behind some nandina bushes next to his house and settled in to take this step toward manhood—as we perceived it at that time. It was a flawed plan from the get-go. First of all, the beer was hot, and it sprayed all over us when we opened it. Secondly, Terry drank about half of his and started throwing up loudly and violently. Next, both our parents smelled beer on us when we went inside that night, forcing us to confess our sins. Lastly, Gaines got grounded for hiding beer in their garage, and then, later that night, he beat the dickens out of Terry for causing all this trouble. Not that it matters, but I finished my beer and liked it. I went on to drink lots of beer in my life, but I always shied away from Falstaff.

Smoking was a noteworthy part of growing up in Marshall in the early 1950s. It never was among the most important things to us boys, but it clearly deserved a mention.

Chapter 11
Girls

I asked Jo Ann Efurd to marry me when I was five years old. She accepted my proposal, and I firmed up our commitment by presenting her with a plastic ring I had found in a box of cereal that very morning. I had met my fiancé the day before as I was exploring the area three blocks from my house on my tricycle. The Efurds were new, short-term renters in our neighborhood, moving into the white frame house across from my good friend Sally Van Wert's house. As I pedaled by their house, I spotted Jo Ann riding her tricycle in their driveway. I brazenly rode up to her, and we sort of just looked each other over for a minute or so. Then we started riding our trikes together. Even though not much was said between us, I was smitten immediately by her beauty, charm and the way she handled her wheels. She was a year older than me, but we didn't let our age difference get in the way of our love of each other. Her mother called her in for a nap, so I pedaled home committed to returning to her the next day to continue our whirlwind courtship. I returned the next day, asked her to marry me, and slipped the ring on her finger when she said "yes."

(L to R) Sally Van Wert, Barbara Worley, Jo Ann Efurd and Billy Worley chill out with ice cream at our neighborhood drug store. Please note Jo Ann and I were engaged for a week when I was five and she was six, making her my first girlfriend ever.

After that, we sort of drifted apart. I guess you could say our relationship fell victim to the great distance between our homes. I have since learned it is very difficult for romance to survive when the lovers are a great distance apart. The three blocks from my house to her house—a bit uphill, too—just made it too hard for me to be able to sustain the courtship.

Also, the Efurds soon moved to their new home on Marshall's Northside. One day I rode up to her house to get my ring back, but they had moved. Jo Ann and I re-established our friendship when we got to junior high. At that time, I asked her if she still had my ring and she said "no." I'm not even sure she remembered our earlier engagement at all. Bummer.

I always liked girls. I never went through that phase in which boys couldn't stand girls. Girls always turned me on; even before I knew what "turned on" meant. I didn't want to play sports with girls or hang out with them all the time, but being in the presence of a pretty girl always fired my rockets.

Early in my first-grade school year, our teacher, Mrs. Robbins, asked us to tell the class what we wanted to be when we grew up. Back then, most of the girls wanted to be teachers or nurses. Most of the boys wanted to be policemen or firemen or soldiers. Me? I was perplexed by the question and struggled with how I should answer it. I was mightily torn between wanting to be a professional baseball player or a shoe salesman. When my turn came to report my plans for the future, I went with shoe salesman. None of my classmates cared about my career choice, but apparently Mrs. Robbins did. She asked me to stay in for a minute when the recess bell rang. When the classroom had cleared out except for the two of us, she asked me why I wanted to be a shoe salesman. I told her I didn't know, but, down deep, I did know why I wanted to be a shoe salesman. I had recently seen a full-page advertisement for some shoe company in the *Saturday Evening Post* magazine in which a male sales-man was slipping a new shoe on some gorgeous lady's foot. She was seated in a chair, and he was seated on a little stool in front of her. He was holding her heel while he eased her foot into the red high heel. Most folks may have focused on the shoe when they looked at the ad, but not me. I totally focused on the lady's beautiful leg. I looked at the picture for some time, and I decided that salesman had a dream job. Mrs. Robbins never found out why I said I wanted to grow up and be a shoe salesman. Life ended up taking me down a different career path, but, even today, I think a shoe salesman has a primo job. All those pretty legs, my oh my.

In one corner of Mrs. Robbins's classroom she had cre-ated a nook she called the library. It consisted of a table with benches on both sides of it that were about six feet long. Lots of first-grade-appropriate books were strewn over the table's surface. Mrs. Robbins would rotate us kids in groups of six in and out of the library. One day, Dianne Applebaum, Johnny Bryant and I were seated on the same bench during "library." Dianne was seated between Johnny and me. No one was pay-ing much attention to the books that day, particularly Johnny. He was focused on getting Dianne to show him her panties. Dianne must have "liked" Johnny because she complied. In fact, she showed her knickers several times. I asked Johnny to get her to show me her panties, and, at his request, she did so. My girlfriend, Ruth Ann, was sitting across from me at the table and I asked her to show me her panties. She looked at me like I was nuts and gave me a firm "no." I guess Dianne liked Johnny more than Ruth Ann liked me. I had no idea why it thrilled me to see the side of Dianne's panties, but it did. Like I said before, I liked girls.

When I started first grade, I took a serious shine to Ruth Ann McClaran the first week of school. Not only was she gorgeous, she was the only first grader—boy or girl—who could keep up with me in a foot race. She lived one block behind me on Wilson Street, and I used to ride my bike back and forth in front of her house, hoping to catch her outside. One day I caught her turning cartwheels in her front yard, and I stopped by for a visit. We chatted awhile, and she giggled at my futile efforts at turning a cartwheel. As our rela-

School Days
1956-57

Ruth Ann was my "true" love for four years in elementary school. What a jewel!

tionship blossomed that afternoon, I worked up the nerve to kiss her on her cheek. I was a fast worker. It was a very quick peck, but we both knew what it meant. It meant we were now girlfriend and boyfriend. The enormity of the moment caused her to turn beet red and caused me to panic and tell her I had to go home. I quickly jumped on my bike and tore out like my pants were on fire. That night at home, I told my brothers about my new girlfriend, and, of course, they teased me mercilessly for years—not days—to come. Unlike my fling with Jo Ann Efurd, my relationship with Ruth Ann lasted for years. In fact, we were "together" until the end of the fourth grade. Over those years, I think I only kissed Ruth Ann's cheek two or three more times. Our school had an annual carnival in May, appropriately enough called May Fete, and part of the carnival was a hayride. Ruth Ann and I always went on the hayride together, and that's where I mustered the courage to put my arm around her and peck her on the cheek for the second time in our maturing romance. Ruth Ann McClaran was my first true girlfriend. Even today, I hold Ruth Ann in a special place in my heart. Also, I still wonder which of us would have won a head-to-head foot race.

During the entire four years Ruth Ann and I were "together," I was only tempted to stray a couple of times. One time, during a first-grade recess, I took special notice of how ravishingly beautiful Kay Wilson was. We hung around together that play period, and I remember being unable to take my eyes off her. She had raven black hair, dark brown eyes and a beautiful tan. She was wearing a bright yellow dress that was trimmed in turquoise rickrack. No doubt about it, she was the total package. That afternoon after school, Charlie Stark and I were sitting under a large oak tree in his yard, and I professed my infatuation with Kay. Her dark hair and eyes, along with her tan skin, prompted me to tell Charlie I was pretty sure she was a Cherokee Indian. I went on to tell Charlie I might even marry Kay someday. The next day, while still an admirer of Kay, I decided I just couldn't live without Ruth Ann in my life, so my near-fling with Kay Wilson was over. I will, however, admit that visions of Kay in the yellow dress still cause a little stir inside of me. I later found out she wasn't a Cherokee Indian. At our fiftieth high school reunion, I confessed my remembrance of her yellow dress and how good she looked in it. She told me her mother had made it for her. Good work, Mrs. Wilson.

In the second grade, I spent about a week thinking Patricia Livingston was very cute. She had a wide grin and was missing her two top-row front teeth. The toothless look looked good on Patricia. She was definitely cute, but my interest in her never took root. Donna Jean Hall moved to our school in the fourth grade and was the object of my unspoken admiration for about two weeks in the fourth grade. She was pretty and had all her teeth. We even exchanged a couple of notes during that time, but our romance never caught fire. Also, Mrs. Parker intercepted one of our notes and embarrassed us both by reading it to the entire class. It was tough for a meaningful relationship to develop when someone had access to our confidential communiqués.

For a few months that year, a really pretty girl named Elaine Pike attended our school. She had honey blonde hair, which looked stunning with her black turtleneck, and she and

I both knew we were a couple without having to verbalize it. She moved to Louisiana soon after our discovery of each other and that was that. It didn't much matter to me, though, because in the end, I was still Ruth Ann's "man." The next year, I heard Elaine had moved back to Marshall and was living in a duplex over by East End Elementary School. One Saturday, I rode my bike to East End, and, after some searching, found her. After visiting with her a while, I decided the spark that had once ignited our romance had fizzled out. I'm pretty sure she felt the same way. I never saw her again.

I don't know what caused Ruth Ann and me to call it quits after the fourth grade. Perhaps three quick smooches on the cheek over a four-year time span weren't enough to keep the flames of passion fanned. Or maybe she thought I was moving too fast. Perhaps she saw me running on the school ground and thought I had lost a step.

At any rate, our split-up left me free to play the field in the fifth grade. I had brief crushes on Lynn Abney, Susie Musser, Patti Dickerson and Nancy Brown, but nothing "stuck." I had a short but rather intense fling with a sixth-grade girl named Leslie Ann Reed. One day at recess she coaxed me into the music annex that was empty at the time and began hugging and kissing me. I told her I had to get back to the kickball game and I burst out of the music room and headed for centerfield. Wow! Her hormones were way ahead of my testosterone at that point. She scared the dickens out of me. I dodged her like all-get-out until she lost interest in me.

Next, Shirley Munden and I started liking each other. Shirley was two years older than me and went to another school. Then my affections turned to Salley Whitener. Neither relationship took off because the only time we saw each other was Saturday mornings at the Paramount Theater's Kiddie Show. Shirley and Salley weren't Southsiders, so the courtships were doomed from the start.

Early in the sixth-grade school year, I fell hard for a cute little blonde named Carol Marshall. She lived thirteen miles south of Marshall on a ranch. Her dad was a cattleman and big-time mink rancher. My first car date was with Carol. We went to the annual dance for students at Mrs. Cowley's dance school. We were taught how to do the box waltz, the jitterbug, the square dance and a host of South American dances. No one talked while dancing because we were all too busy counting steps to ourselves. My mother made a corsage out of camellias from our yard for me to give to Carol. My brother Robert drove us to and from the dance. He was the perfect chauffer because he kept us loose by acting stupid. Without him to create conversation, I don't think Carol or I could have thought of anything to say. The dance and the date went fine, but when we got home from taking Carol home, Daddy complained about the fifty-two miles we put on the car going and coming from Carol's house. He told me to find a new girlfriend—one who lived this side of "over yonder." Of course, my love of Carol overrode Daddy's advice and our romance continued.

It was standard fare for boyfriends and girlfriends to meet at the Kiddie Show at the Paramount on Saturday mornings. It was our way of dating. One Saturday morning, Carol and I were snuggled up in our theater seats staring at whatever was on the screen. After much trepidation, I put my arm around Carol. She accepted my advance and put her head on my shoulder. We had sat through the movie, the serial, and the five or six cartoons that filled the bill for the Kiddie Show when her dad tapped her on the arm and told her it was time to go home. I looked over my shoulder and saw Mr. Marshall looming over us. He was waiting for Carol to disentangle herself from me and leave with him. I was both mortified and scared to death. Mr. Marshall was a huge man who had been a basketball star at Baylor University. To me—at that moment—he looked like Goliath, and I felt like a rockless David. I just knew he was going to rip my head off for having had my arm around his daughter. He offered me a ride home, but I politely declined and kept staring at the screen as though it was the most fascinating thing I had ever seen. The last thing I wanted was to be trapped in a car with an irate Mr. Marshall. They left and, soon thereafter, so did I. I started walking home and had completed about one-third of the two-mile hike when a major, major thunderstorm hit. It was pouring down so hard I couldn't see two feet in front of my nose when, all at once, I hear a car horn toot. I looked over and saw the Marshall's blue and white '56 Buick stopped by the curb. Mr. Marshall leaned across Carol and yelled through an open window for me to jump in so he could take me home. I figured he still had a mad on about me having my arm around Carol so I responded by saying, "No, thank you. I really like to walk in the rain." After I declined two more of his pleadings, he gave up and drove on. I'm sure he thought he wasn't keen on having his daughter end up with a guy this dumb over the long haul.

Early in the sixth-grade school year, the principal and two sixth-grade teachers selected six students to run for student council president. Carol and I were both among the six. The six of us were told we would have to make a campaign speech to a student assembly, and the actual election would take place after that. Realizing the fear of making a speech in front of the entire student body could put us in paralysis, Mr. Phillips told us we would have three full weeks to prepare our speeches. Additionally, each of us would be partnered with another candidate and we would be given thirty minutes each school day leading up to the election to go out on the school ground where we could give each other our respective speeches over and over until we had them down pat. Knowing we had all that time to prepare for speech day seemed to calm us a bit. I was paired with John Tebbetts. I went home and wrote my speech over the weekend, and so did he. I didn't even tell my family about this honor and just quickly scribbled out a rather childlike speech. John, however, co-opted his parents into the campaign and into the writing of the speech.

On the following Monday, John and I went out on the empty playground and started reciting our speeches to each other. The other two pairs of candidates staked out other parts of the playground and were also doing back-and-forth recitations. Carol was paired with Joan Bergstrom. They were over by the seesaws. I read my speech to John, and then it was his turn to read his to me. Once he had done so, I was flabbergasted to the max. I didn't know what half of the words meant, but I knew it was good. His speech sounded like one Winston Churchill would have given to Parliament during the war and that would have gone down as one of his proudest moments. It was a fantastic speech, and mine paled by comparison. But so be it. We practiced together for three weeks, and I knew my speech backward and forward.

Finally, the day of the assembly arrived. It was held in the cafeteria, and we candidates were seated on the raised stage at one end of the room. I was feeling okay about the event until Mr. Phillips called the assembly to order, explained the agenda, and then called on me to speak first. It was like I had been hit between the eyes by a bolt of lightning. I staggered to the podium and held on for dear life. My legs were shaking so bad I thought I was going to pile-up on the floor. When I looked out over the room full of people who were all looking at me, I thought I was going into a full-blown Ben Blue swoon. I couldn't remember a single word from my speech. I was totally blank, but right before I started crying and vomiting, I remembered John Tebbetts's speech. I remembered it word for word. I started giving his speech and, the further I went along, the more I got into it. I gave it beautifully. When it was over, I calmly turned around and went back to my seat, pretending not to notice the glinting daggers John was casting my way from his eyes. Mr. Phillips called on John next. He took the podium, turned back and looked at me, then muttered parts of the speech the audience had just heard. He then meekly drifted back to his chair. To this day, I feel guilty for having stolen John's great speech. I am pleased to report John's election loss didn't traumatize him. He went on to become a highly respected plastic surgeon and even made the national news in the late 1970s by becoming the first American surgeon to successfully reattach a young girl's hand that had been severed in an accident.

When they tallied the votes, Carol and I each had 152 votes and were tied for the election lead. Mr. Phillips decided to break the tie by polling the four sixth graders who hadn't voted because they were at home sick. One of the sick-at-home students was Lynn Abney. She and my best friend Terry were "going steady" at the time so Terry quickly called Lynn and suggested she should vote for me when Mr. Phillips called her. She did vote for me, and I got three of the four votes. I was the new president of the South Marshall Elementary School Student Council—thanks to John Tebbetts's speech and Terry's pull with Lynn Abney. Sorry, John. Sorry, Carol.

Carol and I remained boyfriend-girlfriend until midway through the seventh grade, at which time she "chose" my good friend David Wist over me. He still regularly reminds me of his successful theft of Carol's affections from me back in the seventh grade. Truthfully, I still can't believe she dumped me. Where'd I go wrong, Carol?

In the 1950s, if you were "going steady" with someone, the two of you exchanged disks. A disk was a round, silver piece of jewelry you had your first name engraved on that you put on a chain and presented to your "steady." He or she wore it proudly, proclaiming to all that their heart belonged to whoever's name was on the disk. I found Carol's disk in a box of old memorabilia in 2009, packaged it up, and mailed it back to her. I told her I had finally given up on our reconciliation. I wonder if she sent it to David Wist.

During those formative years, I had "girlfriends" and "friends that were girls." My first friend that was a girl was Sally Van Wert. Our friendship dated back to pre-school

times when I was cruising around the neighborhood on my tricycle. Sally went to kindergarten with Terry, so she was his good buddy before she was mine. He and I used to trike up to Sally's house on a fairly regular basis, mainly because Sally was Terry's true love. They were romantically connected, and I just liked them both. Sally became my go-to girl when I needed to find out who liked who,

Sally could color and she could explain the facts of life to her friend Scotty. She did both.

who didn't like who, and anything else that was happening with girls in South Marshall.

When I was in the fifth grade, I once found three dimes in the parking lot in front of the Food Mart, a neighborhood grocery store. I immediately went inside and headed for the ice cream freezer. I bought me a half pint of Borden's strawberry ice cream, grabbed me a wooden ice cream spoon, and headed up Nathan Street in search of a shade tree under which I could sit and devour my godsend. I chose the big elm that bordered Nathan and was on the edge of the Van Wert's yard. I had no sooner got the lid off my ice cream container when Sally meandered up and sat on the curb beside me. As I took my first bite, Sally calmly said, "Mellie Jo started." I kept waiting for her to tell me exactly what Mellie Jo had started, but Sally just smiled and said nothing. I took another bite of ice cream and inquired about just what Mellie Jo had "started." Sally answered, "Menstruating" (she pronounced it "menistrating") and acted like I should have known without asking. Reading the blank stare on my face, Sally began a mind-numbing explanation of what menstruating meant and how it worked. I was a bundle of confusion, disbelief and shock. Also, my strawberry ice cream didn't look so good anymore, so I just eased it down to the curb by my feet. By the time Sally had finished the female anatomy class and had tied it all in to sex, pregnancy, childbirth and maturity, I had turned white as a sheet, and my ice cream had melted and was oozing toward the storm drain in front of Miss Estelle's house. Sally had done a thorough job, and that little episode changed my life forever. A heaping bunch of my naiveté and little boyishness slipped down that storm drain with my melted strawberry ice cream that afternoon. I couldn't look at Mellie Jo for months, but, other than that, life went right along. Even today, when I'm confounded by a woman's actions, mystery illnesses or odd behavior, I think of calling Sally for an explanation. She would know, and she would tell me. Our friendship was—and still is—like that.

Like I said at the beginning, I've always liked girls a lot. Still do. But a girl named Kay Hightower has now had my disk for more than fifty years.

Chapter 12
Catfish, Collards, Pigs' Feet, and Pinto Beans

I never ate possum as a kid—nor as an adult. I have, on occasion, eaten grits (and loved them), but I still don't know for sure what chitterlings are, and I have never—to my knowledge—eaten them. I point out those things because I was born and raised in East Texas, and, as I have now lived in other parts of our nation, I find that many non-Southerners think those of us who were Southerners ate just about anything as we ran barefooted through the hills dodging education and the government agents trying to shut down our stills. Some of those stereotypes might have a small ring of truth to them, but I'm here to tell you we ate well.

There are some regional preferences when it comes to food, to be sure. However, I find we tend to develop a taste for the foods available to us and may turn up our noses at the things we don't readily have and know nothing about.

For example, we enjoyed catfish while most Northerners thought only rednecks ate catfish. On the other hand, many Northerners loved pike fish. We threw pikes back when we caught them because they were so boney, and we figured they were more trouble than they were worth. At our house, when Mother fried a chicken, we ate the neck, liver, heart and gizzard. I don't think eating necks, livers, hearts and gizzards ever really caught on up north. But I did learn of some Northerners who ate chicken feet and tripe. At this point, I should add I believe eating most of the chicken's parts was likely reflective of our economic situation and Daddy's effort to try to keep three ever-hungry sons full. For those of you who never tried a chicken neck, let me tell you, the underneath portion of the curve in a chicken's neck is some of the best meat the bird has to offer.

Some of the things we ate were a bit weird and not for everybody. Daddy liked pickled pigs' feet and knuckles. They came in a jar floating in a yellowish liquid that smelled like vinegar. It wasn't a pretty presentation, as it's dang near impossible for a pig's foot to be attractive, except maybe to another pig. They didn't taste bad at all, but Daddy had very little competition for his chosen delicacy. Big jars of pickled pigs' feet stood alongside big jars of hard-boiled eggs on the counters of many Southern bars. They sold a lot of them back in the 1950s and probably still do. Maybe that means you have to be half drunk to enjoy them. We also ate our share of SPAM® in the early 50s. I guess lots of our veterans came home with a taste for SPAM after the War. We had SPAM with our toast and eggs, and we had SPAM sandwiches. It was okay, and it was cheaper than bacon, sausage and sandwich meat. Speaking of sandwich meat, we basically had three kinds at our house from which to choose. Baloney (highbrows call it bologna) was the most prevalent at 1301 S. Grove, but we sometimes had pressed ham or goose liver (liverwurst). Oddly enough, I don't remember eating many peanut butter and jelly sandwiches. Was peanut butter expensive back then? I had more PBJ sandwiches at the Weeks's house than I did at my house.

We in the South did seem to have a love affair with big green leaves. In addition to spinach, we ate the dickens out of turnip greens, collard greens and mustard greens, all cooked with salt pork. Our parents sold us on the importance of these greens to our health, and, besides, they tasted good. Some folks enjoyed poke salads, which got that name because they included the green shoots of the pokeweed. One had to be careful when picking poke shoots, because you surely didn't want to let one of the pokeweed's purple berries fall in your bowl. They were highly poisonous. Other leaf-eaters liked dandelion leaves. Can't say I ever ate anything to do with a dandelion, but I might have. All of the aforementioned greens are still popular in East Texas and the South. Just last month, I heard a disc jockey on a Tyler, Texas radio station describe a summer day as "hotter than a pot of collards on a burning stump." Now that's hot, folks.

Our menus at home were strongly influenced by how much things cost. We ate for bulk as much as we did for quality. We had beans, beans and more beans. My life-long friend, David Wist, spent a lot of mealtimes at our house from elementary school through college, and, even today, he says he never remembers us having a meal without pinto beans. Eating all those beans did, however, have a downside. As I mentioned in an earlier chapter, we three boys slept together in one bed, and the South Grove Street Bean Wars were often relentless and brutal. To his credit, I will say, brother Robert never lost a gas battle. If awards had been granted for "deadliest gas," Robert would have claimed The Medal of Honor. On occasion, his murderous clouds even woke Mother and Daddy from dead sleeps, and they were in their own bedroom with the door closed. Mother and Daddy's quest to fill the three of us up included lots of potatoes, bread and gravy, too. Even today, if you give me a skillet full of gravy and a half a loaf of bread, I'll be glad to sop away the hours.

In the mornings, we had orange juice and milk with our breakfast. We drank iced tea by the gallons with lunch and dinner. By the way, we referred to our noon meal as "dinner" and our evening meal as "supper" back then. I'm not sure when we switched over to lunch and dinner, but either works for me. We also called our refrigerator an ice box and our range was just a stove. When Mother or Daddy was at home, there was always a pot of coffee on the stove. They drank it all day and up until bedtime. Daddy had thrown away the coffee pot's innards and would simply boil his coffee. He put broken eggshells in the pot to make the coffee grounds settle to the bottom. It was strong, and he called it "creek-bottom coffee." I don't know if Daddy didn't know how to use a fully intact coffee pot, or if he just preferred his coffee made the way of his youth.

Sometimes, you could find a quart of buttermilk in our ice box. Mother and brother Homer really liked buttermilk. Daddy, Robert and me not so much. We all did like it with crackers crumbled up in it, and it served as a bit of a special treat in that way. We used to crumble up cornbread in it, too. Simply stir it up a bit, and eat it with a spoon. It's not bad, but it's certainly no threat to Starbucks.

Sunday dinner was where Mother kicked it into high gear. Roast beef cooked with carrots, potatoes and onions was a Sunday star at our house. We poured the natural gravy over the meat, the potatoes and bread. A side vegetable of greens, cabbage or green beans added to our enjoyment. Other Sunday meals included a perfect meatloaf served in a skillet full of tomato soup-based red gravy that Mother made with onions, bread crumbs, eggs, milk and other magical ingredients that made it incredibly delicious. When the meal was over, we three boys went through a loaf of bread sopping up the gravy from the skillet. She also sometimes served us a homemade hot tamale pie that was beyond comprehension. She used tamales, chili, cheese, onions, Fritos and just the right amount of ketchup and seasoning to win the day. Unbelievably good. It was brother Robert's favorite meal hands down.

When we had dessert, it was usually one of the following: banana pudding, applesauce or Jell-O. Mother made a to-die-for lemon pie, but it only appeared on special occasions. When our Cub Scout Pack held its big quarterly meetings at the school cafeteria, parents were asked to bring a dessert. The two most popular treats were always Mrs. Warnstaff's pecan pie and Mother's lemon pie. Mother's lemon pie made me proud. For snacks, Mother kept fresh fruit available. She was a big believer in the benefits of fruit to one's health. Whenever I was constipated, Mother gave me prunes. I still don't know how she always knew when I was constipated, but she did. That's when I decided God whispered stuff in parents' ears that He didn't share with kids.

It never really bothered me back then, but I still think about the "goodies" we never had at our house. For example, I NEVER remember there being sodas at our house. Daddy considered them frivolous and too expensive. I do remember that sometimes on a hot day Mother made up a pitcher of Kool Aid for me and my running buddies. On winter afternoons, Mother would occasionally make hot chocolate in her biggest pot. She would heat milk while stirring in the Hershey's chocolate powder and sugar. One time, Homer and Robert came in from playing outdoors, and Homer spotted the "hot chocolate" pot on the stove so he made a beeline to it and started chug-a-lugging it to make sure he got his fill before Robert could get to it. In his greed, he was swallowing without tasting, and all was going well until a dirty dishrag from the bottom of the pan hit him in the mouth. That's when he discovered that he had been drinking filthy water left in the pot from Mother's baseboard cleaning. Needless to say, Robert had the last laugh that day.

Speaking of Robert, he got in trouble with Daddy one time because he got nabbed "smuggling" food to his hound, Belle. It seems Daddy had noticed we were going through lots and lots of eggs, thereby boosting the cost of groceries. When he brought it up one night at supper, Robert instantly looked guilty. When quizzed about the missing eggs by Daddy, Robert fessed-up to feeding Belle three or four raw eggs a day. When pressed for why he had given Belle so many eggs, Robert said it was because it would make Belle's coat rich and shiny. I can't quote Daddy's response to Robert, but it had something to do with making his scrawny butt shiny if he did it again. I got real quiet during this exchange because I had been feeding Belle potato chips. I did it because it was fun to watch Belle try to chew potato chips, and I didn't think Daddy would buy that being a good idea. Thank the Lord, it didn't come up. By the way, Belle really did have the shiniest coat of any dog in South Marshall—for a while anyway.

The only time a cake showed up at our table was when a birthday was being celebrated. In other words, rarely. Cookies, candy, cupcakes, ice cream? Nope. Daddy would splurge every now and then and bring home some mellorine, which was a cheaped-down ice cream substitute. Real ice cream was just too expensive. By the way, I don't recall how "mellorine" was spelled, and it's not in the dictionary. I didn't eat my first piece of French bread until I was out of college. We ate a lot more biscuits than we did rolls because my folks made them from scratch. While we ate lots of fresh fish, which was usually given to us by the Ezells from across the street, we never had seafood. Again, just too expensive. I didn't have my first shrimp until I was in high school. We weren't poor. I think families just lived within their means back in the '50s. I had very few friends back then that had all of those "goodies" in their pantries. Like I said earlier, it didn't bother me. We are well-served to remember there were no credit cards like VISA or MasterCard back then. The inability to charge anything meant that families could only buy those items they could pay for at that time. The availability of credit cards has made everything available to anyone at any time nowadays. It's up to you to decide which alternative is the wisest. Now, I do want to point out we had gasoline company credit cards and a Sears Roebuck credit card, but neither gas stations nor Sears sold groceries.

I think memories of the Depression, along with the War and rationing, taught folks frugal ways and curbed the wasting of food. I just don't remember leftovers being thrown away at our house. Come to think of it, I don't remember there ever being leftovers at our house. The three of us high-energy boys approached any food before us aggressively and thoroughly. Another thing I remember is there were no finicky eaters at our house. We all liked everything. One time I mentioned to Daddy that I didn't really care for beets. He just told me to eat them; they were good for me. I still don't care for beets, but I eat them. They are good for me.

On my tenth birthday, which fell within a day or two of Easter, my cousin Pauline gave me two brightly colored baby chicks. I quickly dubbed them Ike and Mamie in honor of our president and first lady. I loved those chicks and played with them every day after school. As they grew, their colors faded away, and they became a normal hen and a normal rooster.

(L to R) Terry, Eric Wolber, Frank Timmins, Scooter Adams, the guest of honor Scotty, Billy Dixon, Charlie , Clarence, Gary Sims, Maner "Bubba" Jones and Mike Jennings celebrate Scotty's tenth birthday at City Park.

They would still hop up into my lap and stretch their necks while I stroked them. I noticed they were getting too big for the small chicken wire pen we built for them but I figured all I needed to do was to enlarge the pen. Daddy had other thoughts in mind. One afternoon I came home from school and Ike and Mamie were gone. When I put out an Amber Alert on them, Daddy told me he had given them to Hallart, our part-time maid and housekeeper. Daddy explained that since Hallart lived in the country, Ike and Mamie would have plenty of space to roam, making them both very happy. Made sense to me. The next time we went to pick up Hallart for work, I jumped out of the car and ran all around her yard looking for my chickens. They were nowhere to be found. Once in the car with Daddy and Hallart, I asked where Ike and Mamie were. She replied, "We ate them Sunday." Like I said, those were "nothing goes to waste" times, and food was food.

There were some nice cafés and restaurants in Marshall, but we never ate at them. Eating out was very, very rare for our family. It was just "too expensive." Oh, we occasionally bought hamburgers or Brown Pigs, but we never—and I mean never—ate in the nicer restaurants. By the way, Brown Pigs were incredibly delicious pork barbecue sandwiches made with the Neely Family's secret recipe. It was a Marshall specialty in the 1940s and it still is today. To an ex-Marshallite, it is unimaginable to visit Marshall without a visit to Neely's on Grand. The only times I can remember our family dining out were when we were traveling. Basically, we traveled only when we were going to visit family. When we pulled up in front of a roadside café, Daddy always reminded us boys not to order our food until we checked it with him. Of course, that meant he wanted final approval on how much money we spent on our food. That policy was instituted after brother Robert once ordered shrimp without getting Daddy's approval, and Daddy was too embarrassed to cancel the order. When we did go on vacation, we always stayed in motels that had kitchenettes, so we could prepare our own meals. I liked this practice because it led to lots of family picnics.

I experienced some "food firsts" that deserve mentioning. Dick Cole's mother, Miss Dolly, made me my first-ever grilled cheese sandwich. Whoa boy, it was good! My brother Homer bought me my first ice cream sundae when I was eleven. Uncle Blackie treated me to my first root beer float at A&W Root Beer in Alexandria, Louisiana, when I was twelve. Mother, Daddy and I didn't have our first pizza until I was seventeen. Brother Robert bought it for us in the French Quarter when we were in New Orleans for his wedding.

I suppose it's a little odd to have a chapter in my memoirs about food. I think I included it because so many of my non-Texan and non-Southern friends have quizzed me about what we ate growing up in Texas in the 1940s through the 1960s. I prefer to think we were pretty darn normal. Even today, I'm not a good one on which to waste your finest delicacies.

My tastes are simple and lean toward quantity as opposed to quality. I guess my preferences reflect the way I was brought up. Baloney, pinto beans, gravy, bread and potatoes—bring 'em on.

Chapter 13

A Horse in Sunday School and a Swim in the Baptismal

God was big in Marshall and in the rest of the United States in the 1950s. So was unabashed patriotism. There seemed to be a consensus that our America was, in fact, "one nation under God." I was often asked *where* I went to church. I was never asked *if* I went to church. Concerning our near-rabid patriotism, well I guess it was understandable. We had just emerged from World War II, and most of our citizenry were pretty much unified in their love of nation and pride in the role we had played in helping to win the War. Obviously, the unbridled patriotism had crested during the War, but it also flooded into the 1950s. We knew the words to our national anthem, and we stood reverently when we heard it played. Also, we all placed our right hand over our heart during its playing as a symbol of our love of country and respect for those who had died for our freedom. We began each school day with the Pledge of Allegiance, and we began our assemblies and sporting events with a prayer. There were pictures of Washington, Lincoln and Eisenhower hanging in each classroom. This surge of patriotism and national confidence lasted through the Korean War and right up until the one-two punch of the civil rights movement and the hugely unpopular Vietnam War. These two events reminded us we were not in Camelot, and, in fact, the American Way had major warts that demanded our attention.

Many classrooms also displayed posters that proclaimed "In God We Trust" or listed the Ten Commandments. I've not been in a classroom in many years, but I'd bet few, if any, now have visible proclamations of love of God. While the neutering of our schools may have been considered necessary to some, it didn't get high marks from me. Having God and patriotism in our classroom gave me a sense of having membership in two very big and important "clubs." I enjoyed my membership in both clubs, and I believe my exposure to the ideals espoused by each helped me develop healthy, fortifying feelings of self-worth and a keen sense of my responsibilities to God, my country and to my fellow man.

I've often wondered if we removed the word "God" from the Ten Commandments and contemporized them a bit, who could dispute the wisdom of their content? Instead of calling them the Ten Commandments, what if we dubbed them "Ten

Suggestions for Better Living"? Try these on and see what you think:

1. Don't make people, animals or things into gods— it's unhealthy and you will be disappointed;

2. Don't bow down to statues, pictures or things made from elements such as gold—it's a waste of time;

3. Don't cuss—using anyone's name in vain does no one any good;

4. Take Sundays off—everyone needs a day to rest, re-charge their batteries and focus on the good side of life;

5. Be nice to your Mom and Dad—you owe them your life, so make them proud;

6. Don't kill anyone—it's just not nice;

7. Keep your legs crossed and your fly zipped up— fooling around will get you in trouble;

8. Don't steal—if it isn't yours, leave it alone;

9. Don't lie—if you do, it'll come back to haunt you; and,

10. Don't waste time being envious—if you want more, work harder or marry wealth.

Every one of these "new" commandments or suggestions offers sage advice on how to live your life and be a better citizen. Maybe we should print up posters itemizing The Ten Suggestions and hang them in classrooms, courthouses, bus stations, etc. Who would be offended?

Our family attended the First Baptist Church in Marshall. It was one of the largest churches in town, so lots of my friends and their families also attended First Baptist. Marshall was mainstream Bible Belt, so our little town had fundamentalists tripping over each other. The fundamentalist voting bloc kept our county "dry," which meant all our closet drinkers had to drive more than twenty miles to "wet" Longview to buy their joy juice and more than twenty miles back to "dry" Marshall after having acquired it or consumed it. Our "dryness" program was a good one if its goal was to keep our local drunks on the highway. Preachers and bootleggers were about the only folks who truly thought keeping Harrison County dry was a good idea. On more than one occasion, I remember riding with my daddy to an isolated spot just off Gum Springs Road where he would park the car, walk about fifty yards into the woods and retrieve his fifth of Early Times from behind a decaying log. He would always leave his payment under a rock near the log because it was imperative that one stay in the good graces of his bootlegger.

Our church's fundamentalism sometimes got in the way of the social life I envisioned for myself. I quickly realized First Baptist leaned toward being a church of "don'ts" as opposed

to being a church of "do's." Once, when I was about eleven
or twelve, I got all excited because our Sunday School class
leaders told us we were going to have a hayride and wiener
roast on a Friday night. Our class had about thirty or so kids
in it, roughly half of whom were girls. Between learning of
the hayride/cook-out and the actual night of the shindig,
I seriously agonized over which girl I would try to cuddle up
with on the hayride. I got the list of candidates down to two.
As Tennessee Ernie Ford used to say, I was "as nervous as a
frog on the freeway with his hopper broke" about whether I
would be able to "hook-up" with the object of my adoration.
When Mother dropped me off at the hayride starting spot,
I spotted two hay wagons, each harnessed up to its own tired
horse. When I saw the two wagons, I had a knot spring up
in my stomach, sensing there could be trouble in paradise.
My greatest fears were realized when Mr. Graham told me
one wagon was for the girls and one was for us boys. I was
stunned. The thought of having to endure the hayride sitting
next to Jimmy, Tommy, Bob, Jesse, Wayman, Tuck, Larry or
any other boy, when Ruth Ann, Dolly, Beverly, Susan, Glenda
and Peggy were in quarantine on wagon #2 was just shocking.
I had wasted hours plotting about how to "make hay" with a
cute girl only to be frustrated by the Baptist doctrine that kept
boys away from girls. From that point on, I stopped going to
church-sponsored youth social gatherings. I also tried to get
Mother and Daddy to join the First Methodist Church. They
had dances, real hayrides and other youth activities they

shared together. They could hold hands without feeling like they were going to hell or being told they were disappointing God. By the way, it didn't escape my keen eye that the children of the very church leaders that preached the evils of dancing were all enrollees in Mrs. Cowley's dance class just like me and all the Methodist kids.

Across the street from our First Baptist Church was Marshall's Episcopal Church. They were doctrinally more liberal than us Baptists, and they were a burr under our leadership's saddle. When they decided to build a big, new fellowship hall between their sanctuary and our church, you would have thought the Devil himself had asked the city for a building permit. Our preacher and deacons, knowing the new building would host youth dances and alcohol-serving wedding receptions, "took to the pulpit." Their project was quickly labeled "the dance hall," and our leaders pounded the pulpit and loudly proclaimed that Satan was setting up camp in our front yard. Our outrage blazed awhile but sort of faded away as their new "sin center" took shape. Since lightning didn't strike the new structure, I guess He wasn't all that upset with it. I didn't think less of our leadership for standing up for their beliefs, but I didn't think any less of the Episcopalians for building their building either. I did question our leaders when I found out our deacons all "adjourned" to Jobe's drug store down the block for coffee every Sunday after they got everyone "ushered" in for the service. Either Jobe's coffee was out of this world, or hypocrisy had taken root in our Narthex.

The bunch of boys I started attending Sunday School with at age five were, for the most part, the same boys I attended Sunday School with through high school. We were all pretty normal, average kids—except for Wayman Lewis. Wayman? Well, Wayman was just flat-out different. He lived three miles outside of town and his parents dropped him off for Sunday School every Sunday morning. I've never been certain whether Mr. and Mrs. Lewis brought Wayman to Sunday School every Sunday because they wanted their boy to get a good Christian education, or because it gave them a couple of hours of Wayman-less peace and quiet. His energy, noise level and disruptiveness were unbridled and endless. He was a load. He was a barrel-chested chubby kid with exceedingly high energy who intimidated kids and adults alike. The gentler boys in our class were scared to death of Wayman. His aggressiveness caused most of the boys to seek a refuge in which they could cower. I suspect old Wayman Lewis was the sole reason Ritalin was invented.

All the youth education classrooms were on the second floor of an old wooden building attached to the rear of our new, fancy church building. One entered the education building from the outside. Once you entered the building, you had to go up about ten to twelve wooden stairs that emptied into a wide, wood-floored hallway. Classrooms were on both sides of the hallway. One Sunday morning, we had just settled into our little classroom when all hell broke out on the stairs and in the hall. It sounded like a herd of buffaloes was stampeding down our hallway. It was worse than that. Wayman Lewis had ridden his large white plow horse up the stairs and into the hallway. Wayman's hollering, his scared horse's neighing, and the reverberating sounds of four prancing hooves on plank floors brought our Baptist world to a screeching stop. All the girls were screaming, and all the male teachers were yelling at Wayman to get himself and "the horse he rode in on" out of the education annex. Wayman just howled with laughter and kept nudging his horse toward the entrance to our small classroom. When he and his steed got to the classroom door, the old horse peered into our crowded little classroom and threw on the brakes. Despite Wayman's efforts to spur the horse on, the horse balked and began a nervous dance that ended with it keeling over right in the doorway. The teachers put Wayman in isolation and finally calmed the horse enough to coax it to its feet and lead it back outside where they tied it to the gas meter on the side of the building. Calm, reverence and order had left the building with Wayman's grand entrance. All of us kids were herded into an assembly room where we sung old hymns until the dismissal bell rang and we were excused. I never heard whether Wayman had ridden his horse to Sunday school with his parents' permission, or if he had rustled the old mare and marched her the three-plus miles to First Baptist without his parents' knowledge.

The horse-in-the-church episode soon passed into history, and our Sunday School class got pretty much back to normal. When we were about eleven or twelve, we had a wonderful teacher named Mr. Thompson. Mr. Thompson was a bit fractious by nature, so it was only natural that Wayman made him jittery during class. He managed to cope fairly well—at least until Wayman started taking money from the offering plate. Our classes always opened with a teacher-led prayer followed by the passing of the offering plate or basket. Each attendee would drop his nickel, dime or quarter into the basket and pass it to the next guy. This collection system worked well for years, until Wayman discovered the joy of taking money out of the basket as opposed to putting his offering into the basket. The boys in the class that witnessed the robbery each Sunday were afraid to tell Mr. Thompson, so the pilfering went on for several weeks. Finally, Mr. Thompson caught Wayman in the act and set out to put a stop to the thievery. The next Sunday morning, Mr. Thompson pulled me aside before class and told me to sit next to Wayman and to stop him from taking money from the basket if he attempted to do so. Mr. Thompson told me he drafted me for the "Wayman-job" because Wayman was a little afraid of me and would stop the stealing if I told him to quit it. Well, sure enough, Wayman put in a nickel and took out a quarter. When I told him to put the quarter back in the basket, he refused and asked me what I intended to do about it. I then whispered my intentions into his ear. He thought for a moment, looked at me for a second and put the quarter back in the basket. From then on, I had to sit next to Wayman every Sunday morning until he stopped stealing from God.

Part of being a "good" Baptist boy or girl was to attend Vacation Bible School (VBS) each summer. It was held on the church grounds for a week each June and was really quite fun. We did arts and crafts and had ice cream and cake or watermelon each day. I'm sure we had a Bible lesson each day also, but I most remember the art and the food. Students from East Texas Baptist College (now a university), a small four-year institution we called "the preacher factory" that was about a mile from our church, usually ran our VBS. One summer, the student who taught our age group was Dot Jones. Dot was a real sweetheart and pretty to boot. One day she gathered us all around a table and was demonstrating some artsy-craftsy thing we were to do with a small piece of copper when we heard a giggle rising from under the table. When we all looked under the table, we found Wayman lying on his back looking up and giggling. When Dot asked him what he was doing, he cheerfully told her he was looking up her skirt. He wasn't being devious. He was just being Wayman.

Baptism in our church was a big, big deal. It was a joyful yet solemn ceremony. When I was twelve, I walked down the aisle and told the preacher I accepted Christ as my savior and wanted to be baptized in His name. We referred to that as "answering the call" at our church. Over the next few weeks, those of us who had answered the call attended a few classes instructing us on the importance of the step we had taken and the significance of our impending baptism. In our church, the baptismal—the tank full of water in which we would be submerged—was high above the choir and visible to all in our large auditorium. When the Sunday of my baptism arrived, I, along with the six or seven others who had answered the call, were lined up on one end of the baptismal in the order the preacher would call us to the front of the tank where he would receive us and physically dunk us while he pronounced the ceremonial words that would make it all official. We had been well-coached on how it would all work, and it would have come off without a hitch if Wayman Lewis hadn't been one of the six or seven in line for the action. We went in alphabetical order, and with my last name beginning with an "E," I was second in line. Wayman Lewis was fourth in line. When the preacher called our name, we were to calmly wade the six or so feet to him, let him take hold of us, and hold our breath when he laid us backward into the water. When he had said his bit, he was then to raise us from the water, and we were to slowly wade out of the other end of the baptismal. Brother Harris would then call the name of the next dippee, and the process would repeat itself until all had been baptized. Simple enough, huh? Nope. Everything went according to plan until the Right Reverend Brother Harris called the name of Wayman Lewis. For undetermined reasons, Wayman decided to swim to the preacher rather than wade to him. By the time Wayman made it to the preacher's side, the baptismal waters were so roiled by his breaststrokes they were sloshing over the edge of the tank and drenching the back two rows of our robe-clad choir down below. Everything sort of stopped in the church as everyone stared at the baptismal with mouths agape and waited for the turbulent waters to calm themselves. Once order was restored, Reverend Harris baptized Wayman and then personally escorted him out of the other end. He then returned to the front of the baptismal and got on with the baptizing.

As an aside, I remember wondering if anyone had ever drowned while being baptized. It seemed a distinct possibility to me because most Texas Baptist preachers talked with a slow Texas drawl and were notoriously long-winded. The fact that some poor believer's lungs might be about to explode while being held under water, would seldom—if ever—deter a spirit-filled preacher from delivering his highly charged message to its glorious end, no matter how long it took. As another aside, I always wondered why sprinkling wasn't good enough for Baptists and a number of other denominations that tended toward fundamentalism. It seemed to work just fine for certain denominations. Did we have to be completely submerged and held under for a while to make sure ALL our sins were washed off of us? Were we just being thorough in case we were a little "sinnier" than others? I'm really surprised we weren't scrubbed down with Lava soap during the process. Lava would remove grease, oil and the outer layer of your skin, so it would surely remove any hard-to-get-off sin that clung to us. Just a thought.

Wayman Lewis was a good kid who became a good man. I'm glad our childhood pre-dated Ritalin, Prozac, Lexapro and such. If it had been around when we were kids, Wayman would have been mainlining it, and I would be walking around today without all the wonderful memories I have thanks to his harmless, yet sometimes shocking, antics. I sometimes think God put Wayman in our church to provide us with some badly needed relief from the doctrinal intensity that near smothered us under a blanket of guilt.

Churches have always needed money to operate. Bills and salaries had to be paid, and an energized church needed monies to fund its outreach program. Doing good deeds and spreading the gospel cost money. Our church paid well and prided itself in having an aggressive outreach program, so the "dig deep and fork it over" plea at the end of our services always came at you hard. Each call for generosity seemed to me to be near perfectly crafted pleadings comprised of well-blended appeals to my need to be thankful for what God had given me, my need to share my good fortune with those less fortunate, and my knowledge that God would be really hacked off at me if I hoarded His blessings. Those calls for my money were well-orchestrated assaults on my senses and my heartstrings—and they worked like a charm on me.

One Sunday, when I was about eight or nine, I was sitting in church with Mother and Daddy and I was so touched by Mr. Hillyard's stewardship message I felt I just had to share my "wealth" with others. The problem was, I just had no wealth to share. I didn't even have a penny. As the offering plate made its way toward me, I found a solution. When the plate came to me, I put my brand new Cub Scout ring in the plate and passed it on down the pew. Riding home from church, Mother noticed I wasn't wearing my ring and asked why I wasn't. I told her I had put it in the offering plate. Daddy pulled the car over, stopped it, and asked me to tell him again where my new ring was. I repeated my story, and Daddy calmly turned the car around and drove back to the church. He parked in the shade of an oak, got out and disappeared into the church. Mother and I sat in the car. He came back a few minutes later and handed me my ring.

Baptist churches were forever having revival meetings. Usually, a revival meeting featured a traveling evangelist who came in and preached for a week. I guess he got a share of the take, because the zeal with which he came after your money was at least as intense as the message we received each Sunday. One week, we had a revival featuring the well-known evangelical brothers Charles Forbes Taylor and Laurie Forbes Taylor. They were born in England but had moved to the United States when they were young and had become quite famous as preachers. Charles was the preacher and Laurie was a fantastic pianist and composer of spiritual songs. When he was four years old and still living in England, Charles had preached to two-thousand worshippers in London. He became known in the British press as "Happy Charlie" because he was always smiling. He and Laurie crafted the perfect blend of entertainment, humor and hardcore gospel preaching. Our church was packed all five nights of their visit. Charles's preaching, Laurie's music and Charles's call for financial support hit home with me. When they started passing the plate, I faced my recurring dilemma. I wanted to give but I had no money. I knew I couldn't give my Scout ring, so what was I to do? As the plate came to me, I ripped out my cuff links and dropped them in the plate. History repeated itself when, on the way home, Mother noticed I was missing my cuff links. We turned around, went back to church and Daddy retrieved my cuff links. From that point on, I was given a quarter to drop in the offering plate each Sunday.

Going to church in the 1950s and early 1960s was a big part of living in a small town. Your attendance was expected and your absence was noted. Folks got all "gussied up" for church. Kids had clothes for everyday living, and they had "church" clothes. You had your everyday friends, and you had your "church" friends. Church attendance was darn near mandatory. You mainly went because you were trying to lead and live a better life. You sometimes went because you knew if you missed a couple of Sundays in a row, somebody from the church would be knocking on your door to lay a pile of guilt at your feet.

Different denominations ran their services in their own unique ways. Some sprinkled; some darn near drowned you. Some had musical instruments; some didn't. Some congregations hollered "Amen!" throughout the service, and some sat there like they were at a funeral. Some knelt, some sat, and some stood. All those variations in worship style left me with the feeling there may be more than one way to get to Heaven. Occasionally, my daddy would load my brothers and me in the car and drive us to the service held at the Galilee Baptist Church. They were held in a small, air-conditioner-less, white wooden building that was located about ten to twelve blocks from our house. Because of the East Texas heat and the fervor created by their worship, the windows were open during services and you could hear it for many blocks. I don't know if Holy Rolly is the proper name for a denomination's style of worship, but that's what everyone in Marshall called Galilee's. Congregations were divided by race in Marshall in the 1950s, and Galilee was a black congregation. Back in those days, Negroes were not allowed in most White churches, but Whites attending Negro churches were welcomed, or at least tolerated. When we entered the Galilee Church, we generally sat at the back of the church on Coke crates that were used for overflow crowds. The entire service was conducted at full throttle. The preaching was handled by a suited preacher who used no notes and roamed the front of his church like a hungry tiger. He was a master at building a congregational frenzy in which members of his flock yelled amens, words of encouragement and spontaneous words of praise for the Lord. Some would stand and talk in tongues, while others would be overcome by the Spirit and faint. When fainting occurred, ladies in the church would rush to the fallen and fan them back to life with the small paper fans with wooden handles they all had. Also, it was not unusual for some worshippers to fall into the aisles and roll around in an emotional outpouring. I guess that's where they got the name "Holy Rollers." The only time you could catch your breath was when the preacher called for music. The respite didn't last long, because the piano and electric guitar were quick to keep the fires burning with inspired, loud versions of old spirituals the words of which everyone knew. The singing was Heaven-inspired and kept the tears flowing. As a young boy, I always left the Galilee service inspired and feeling closer to God. It was a spectacle, to be sure, but it felt so real that I shall never forget the wonderful glow it created in me. I later found out that my friends David and Bobby Wist, who lived about two blocks from Galilee Baptist, used to sneak down to it and hide under the church so they could enjoy the music. I'm sad to report Galilee Baptist was either torn down or fell down. It should have been preserved as an important historical site, because it was a star in Marshall's Christian crown.

Wherever you sat every Sunday in church was your real estate. Everyone sat in the same place every service. When visitors came to First Baptist, they caused a mild disruption because they inevitably sat in "someone's" seat. Everyone was gracious about the encroachment but was quick to reclaim their real estate the following week. Our family always sat on the far left of the chapel, about ten rows down from the back. Mr. and Mrs. Pace and their son Charlie sat three rows behind us. I remember where they sat because Mr. Pace didn't sing along with the hymns; he whistled along with them. He was a gifted whistler, and I loved hearing him. He was a postman in Marshall and was known as the "whistling mailman" because he whistled his way through his route every day. The Paces lived across the street from us, and he always whistled when he worked in his yard. He made our church, our neighborhood and our town happier places through his whistling.

I darn sure didn't grow up under a halo. With some regularity, I strayed from all the churching I had received from all my wonderful, caring teachers. Even as an adult, common Christian sense has spent an inordinate amount of time on the back burner of my life. However, as bad as I was as a kid, as bad as I've been as an adult, and as bad as I am as an old man, I can 100 percent guarantee you I would have been worse without the teachings I received from Sunday School teachers such as Mrs. Power, Mrs. Fowler, Mrs. Hill, Mr. Power, Mrs. Roundtree, Mr. Scott, Mr. Graham and Mr. Thompson. They made a difference in my life. I loved them then, and I love them now.

It's hard to write a chapter dealing with God and patriotism. Both subjects require me, as the writer, to delve deeply into who I am and why I am, and then to reveal those inner feelings to lots of folks I really don't know all that well. Well, I am an unabashed, cross-waving Christian and an unabashed, flag-waving patriot. Love of both God and country were ingrained in me from day one. I cannot imagine life without them.

Chapter 14

A Blue Wool Coat, Frosty's Booger, and Upside-Down Cacti

We weren't poor, but money was always tight. Raising three big, fast-growing, ever-hungry, athletic boys presented a financial challenge to Mother and Daddy. Feeding us, or more specifically, filling us up, was like painting the Golden Gate Bridge—a never-ending chore. We ate lots of beans, gravy and bread, and anything else that had a shot at swelling up inside our bellies and making us think we were full. When I reflect on those times, I cannot recall ever leaving the table hungry. In truth, however, I also seldom remember ever feeling belly-poppin' full. My older brothers, Homer and Robert, went to their graves thinking I had a tapeworm with an insatiable appetite for any and all foods. Even to this day, I cannot name a food I didn't—or don't—like. Well, maybe beets.

Besides trying to fill us up, our parents had to clothe us. Common sense dictated that hand-me-downs were a part of Mother's clothing plan. Since there were no hand-me-downs available to Homer, the oldest of the three of us, he got new clothes. Robert, who was two-and-a-half years younger than Homer, got a few hand-me-downs. However, in most cases, Homer had worn his duds slap-out, leaving them too shoddy for Robert's use. I was ten years younger than Robert, so I didn't have to deal with clothes my older brothers had outgrown. I did, however, occasionally find myself on the receiving end of hand-me-downs from the Cole family, who lived across the street from us. The Coles, like the Eubankses, had three sons: Henry, John and Dickie. Dickie was only three years older than me, so I sometimes got a "goodie" from his closet. As I mentioned before, my first Cub Scout shirt was Dick's old one, which had been John's, which had probably been Henry's before that. One winter, when I was about ten, Mrs. Cole gave me a navy blue, wool, knee-length coat that had helped the three Cole boys survive a lot of East Texas winters. I was quite proud of my new coat. It was ultra-warm, but the thing about it that most impressed me was that it had big, really deep pockets. Those big, deep pockets played a role in an episode of my childhood I would just as soon forget.

One winter day on my way home from school, I wandered into The Food Mart, a smallish neighborhood grocery store owned and operated by a really nice man named Gerald. Gerald had started in The Food Mart as a butcher, but had managed to buy the store from its long-time owner, Mr. Skaggs, who had gone out on Pine Crest Drive and opened Marshall's first 7-11- styled store called Min-A-Pak. Gerald and his Food Mart had a tough row to hoe. The big chains like Safeway, A&P and Piggly Wiggly that had recently come to town beat him on size of inventory and prices, and convenience stores like Min-A-Pak and Pak-A-Sak beat him on, well, convenience. I'm ashamed to say I didn't help Gerald that wintry day I came in off the street wearing my Cole hand-me-down coat. I regularly dropped into The Food Mart to check out their candy stock and see if they had any baseball cards or other interesting new items such as tops, firecrackers, yoyos or marbles. Most of the time when I visited the store, I was just a looker because I seldom had any money. The day I'm telling you about was one of those "just looking" days. I had just about finished my "rounds" when I caught a glimpse of shine and sparkle out of the corner of my eye. A close-up inspection revealed a display of packages of the most beautiful marbles I had ever seen. They were called "cat's eyes" and they were brand-spanking new to the marketplace. It was love at first sight. The cat's eyes were clear glass marbles with little artistically-shaped ribbons of bright color(s) suspended in their centers. I lovingly looked at every pack in the display at least twice, fondling each one of the small, round little beauties through the plastic packaging. What happened next was purely the work of the devil. Three powerful factors—the beauty of the marbles, my being broke, and the big and deep pockets of my new, blue wool coat—converged on me with a vengeance. As if in a trance, I grabbed two of the packages and crammed one down into my coat's left pocket and the other one deep into the shadowy confines of my new coat's right pocket. I then headed for the exit. I was just about to push through the door when Gerald said, "Scotty, are you gonna pay me for those marbles?"

I, of course, replied, "What marbles?"

Gerald then said, "The ones you put in your pocket."

My face felt like it was on fire, and I know my eyes were as big as bike tires, but I somehow managed to stupidly ask, "Which pocket?"

Gerald then walked over to me from behind the counter and fished the marbles out of my right pocket. I was nabbed! Instantly, I had visions of me going to prison, me getting a horrible whoopin' from Daddy and me being exposed as a thief to all my loved ones and friends. However, when I told Gerald I had no money, he just gave me a stern, but non-bruising lecture, and told me, "Get your little butt on home." I tucked my head, left The Food Mart, turned right on Nathan Street and headed home—fully aware of the fact that I still had a package of Gerald's cat's eyes in my left pocket. I guess you might say I had pulled off the "perfect crime." In truth, it was only perfect if you didn't suffer from intense, relentless guilt for years to come. I did. I suffered until I was in my 30s, when on a visit to my home town, I decided to pay Gerald for the marbles I had had in the left pocket of my hand-me-down blue wool coat. Gerald had retired and I couldn't track him down, but I found his grown son working in a small convenience store/gas station. I told the son of my crime against his dad and of my desire to put things right. He reached his dad by phone and then put me on the line. I re-introduced myself to Gerald, confessed my crime and apologized as best I could. He claimed to remember me, but said he didn't remember the "great marble heist" I had pulled off at The Food Mart nearly thirty years earlier. When I told him I wanted to pay him for the marbles, he just chuckled and said it wasn't necessary. It may not have been necessary to him, but it was to me. I gave his son ten dollars and asked him to give it to his dad for me. I hope and suspect he did give the tenner to his dad, but, if he didn't, he would have to live the guilt now because mine was finally cleansed from my soul.

I actually got my clothes from three different sources. Thanks to the Cole boys, I received some hand-me-downs, as I said, but Mother and Daddy also bought me new clothes. I also got quite a few new clothes that had arrived at Sears, Roebuck & Company but were discovered to have some flaw or irregularity that made them unsellable. When these "irregulars" were discovered, Sears would mark them way down and give employees first dibs on buying them. Since Mother was head of the Boys Department at Sears, and Mrs. Cole worked in the Boys Department alongside her, a lot of those "irregulars" made it to our respective homes. Usually, the flaws were pretty hard to spot, so Dick Cole and I usually wore the clothes without the fashion police even noticing. I do, however, remember Mother bringing home a new flawed shirt for me to try. It was long-sleeved and had blue Saguaro cacti all over it. I instantly liked it and couldn't wait to try it on. It was a great fit, and, as I stood before the mirror admiring how I looked in it, Mother pointed out that all of the cacti were upside down. I thought about it a minute, and decided I looked so good in it the upside-down cacti didn't matter all that much. I wore it proudly until I outgrew it, and no one ever said a word about my inverted cacti.

Most of the flawed clothes just had a pocket that was sewn on a little crooked, one sleeve a bit shorter than the other, a bit of discoloring or a pant leg that was shorter than its counterpart. I remember getting an "irregular" sweatshirt with Frosty the Snowman on its front that I just loved. I never knew what was irregular about it until my brother, Robert, pointed out that a screen-printing mistake made it look like Frosty had a big booger dangling from his button nose. I remember Nancy Brown telling me she liked my sweatshirt, so, if Nancy didn't see the booger, I figured others wouldn't either. I liked my Frosty sweatshirt so much I wore it on picture day in the first grade.

Since both of my brothers had passed the six-foot-tall mark by the time they were fifteen, I guess Mother and Daddy had been "burned" by having them outgrow their clothes before they were broken-in good. As a result, they seemed hell-bent on buying me clothes I could "grow into." While I couldn't argue with their logic, I didn't like the end result of their "grow into" policy. It seemed to me I spent an inordinate amount of time in clothes that were just plain too big for me. No one wore shorts back then except a boy named Bill who lived on the other side of town and took voice lessons. It was jeans, and only jeans, with corduroys being acceptable in the winter. When I got new jeans, I had to tighten my belt so much to keep them up that it looked like they were being held up by a drawstring. Also, the legs of the jeans were always four or five inches longer than they needed to be, so I had to roll them up a bunch—not one or two rolls, but six or seven. This situation was tolerable except sometimes when I was running flat-out across the schoolyard, they would come unrolled midstride and the excess denim would get tangled up with the soles of my sneakers, causing some hellacious falls and tumbles. Along about the time I was in the fifth or sixth grade, it became unfashionable to roll your britches legs up. Instead, you had to tuck any excess length up inside your pants legs. Since that change in fashion didn't cause my parents to alter their "grow into" policy, I had to start tucking instead of rolling. Let me tell you, four or five inches of new, thick, tucked denim is terribly uncomfortable rubbing against your calves and much less secure than four to five inches of rolled excess denim. The playground falls just kept on coming. Those falls often produced torn jeans or corduroys. When tears occurred, Mother simply repaired them with iron-on patches, which wasn't really the look you were going for. It was hard to be a stud when you were always tugging, rolling or tucking on your patched jeans. By the way, Mother and Daddy were right. I hit the six foot mark on my fifteenth birthday.

I never heard the word "sneakers" associated with shoes until I was an adult. Our canvas shoes with rubber soles were all called tennis shoes in the 1950s and 1960s, and, to the best of my memory, were mostly made by either Converse or Keds. They were also all of the high-top variety until the mid-to-late '60s, at least in Marshall, Texas. In elementary school, most of us just had two, maybe three, pairs of shoes. In my case, I had a pair of tennis shoes for school and a pair of leather shoes for church and other dress-up events. My "good" shoes usually came from Buster Brown and could only be worn on special occasions. My tennis shoes could be—and were—worn for all playing, exploring, wading, climbing, kicking, etc. We wore our tennis shoes until they were slick on the bottom, tongueless, our toes burst through them or they stunk so bad Mom or Dad threw them away. Getting a new pair of "tennies" was a big deal. There was no doubt in my mind that I could run much faster and jump much higher in new tennis shoes than I could in my old ones. I felt invincible in new tennis shoes. The tread design on the bottom of the new tennies was also important. One was always interested in the design of the footprint left in the dirt by new tennies. When I got new shoes, I would seek out soft dirt so I could leave clear footprints and then step back and admire the tread design.

One time in the third grade I got a new pair of tennis shoes. The first day I wore them to school, I couldn't wait for recess to come so I could get out on the playground to test my theory about being able to run faster and jump higher than I could wearing my old shoes. I decided to show off my new speed by running under a row of elm trees that bordered the school ground. I chose that route because grass wouldn't grow under the elms and it was, therefore, a dirt track. Running on dirt appealed to me for two reasons. First, it meant that after my sprint, I could go back and see if my new tennies left any cool tread imprints in the dust. Second, I wanted to set my new speed record in a place that generated a cloud of dust as I dashed to the end of the elm row. As I prepared to start my speed demo, I casually glanced around to make certain I had an audience. All systems were go, so I put it in drive and took off. I was flying! I was running so fast I decided to look over my shoulder to see if I was leaving a dust trail. Big mistake. While looking for my jet stream, I tripped over a protruding elm root and did a face-first dive into the gravel-filled dirt that seemed to last forever. When I finally came to a stop, I realized I was bleeding from all over my face. Of course the sight of my own blood set me to howling at the top of my lungs. The very kids I had hoped to impress all ran over to me and stood around me staring at the bloody, screaming, failed racer I had become. Mrs. Patterson ran over, got me to my feet and took me into the nurse's office for diagnosis and treatment. The nurse washed off my cuts and scrapes and decided I didn't need any stitches. She dabbed my bleeding spots with hydrogen peroxide, then covered them with iodine and bandaged the spots that needed it. She made me lie down for an hour or so and then pronounced me ready to return to class. When I entered the classroom, I instantly became the object of everyone's stares and winces. In that hour in the nurse's office, my lips had swollen up and had crusted over with dried blood, the iodine had turned bright orange and the multiple bandages made it look like I had had a face transplant—or, perhaps, needed one. When Mother got home from work late that afternoon, she found me sitting on the living room floor playing with my baseball cards. When she saw the sorry state I was in, she gasped, sat down next to me and asked what had happened. I told her it was all because she bought me that new pair of tennis shoes.

About a month before school ended each year, baseball-playing boys started getting fired-up for the nearing Little League season. Little League was for boys from nine to twelve years of age, but one had to go through tryouts and "make" a team. Far more boys tried out and didn't make a team than those who did make one. In those days, there were winners and losers. Even if one made a team, he would ride the bench if his skills weren't good enough to earn him playing time. There were no "everyone must play" rules in the 1950s. Only the winners got their team photo in the paper and there were no trophies. Very few nine-year-olds made a team, but I was one who did. I was a proud member of the Giants. Once you made a team, you were on that team through age twelve. At thirteen, one had to try out for a new team in the Babe Ruth

League which was for ages thirteen to fifteen. There was no stigma attached to not making a team, but making a team definitely gave a boy strutting privileges. At the start of each season, your dad took you to Logan and Whaley—the only sporting goods store in Marshall—and bought you a new pair of Little League baseball shoes. They were solid black and just like big-league baseball shoes except they had rubber cleats instead of metal cleats. Once a boy got his cleats, he put away his tennies and strutted around his school, playground and neighborhood in his cleats. He also got his new team cap and he only took it off when he slept, bathed, or his mother made him do so when he was inside. I never could prove it, but I was pretty sure every girl in South Marshall thought I was hot stuff when they saw me in my cleats and Giants cap. Probably not, though.

Although there weren't very many style choices in kid's clothing back in the 1950s, it was still important that we wore clothes that were "in." Most style changes I remember were gradual and modest—until Elvis Presley hit the scene. Elvis "rocked" our sixth-grade fashion world with his look, demeanor and moves. The thug look was "in." Inspired by the King, long, greasy hair with ducktails replaced crew cuts as the rage, and black leather or vinyl motorcycle jackets became a "must" for the hep cats. The more zippers you had on your jacket the better. Black was the color of choice. One night, Carol Padget had a bop party at her house and eight boys—including me—showed up. Seven of us wore black turtlenecks. Tuck Kemper wore a white turtleneck. We all did a little bopping and jitterbugging but spent the majority of our time combing our hair and slouching around on her front porch just looking cool. Make no mistake about it, we were cool . . . well, as cool as you could be when you arrived at the party on your J. C. Higgins bicycle. In retrospect, I think we all longed to be a perfect combination of Elvis, James Dean and Marlon Brando. I tended to look more like Jerry Lewis than any of those three cats.

I don't really remember giving a hoot whether a kid was rich or poor, dressed in style or didn't. Richard Scott and Roger Kiel often wore sleeveless undershirts to school, but no one cared or teased them. It just didn't matter. As I look back, it was nice being non-judgmental. I wonder when and why we—and more specifically, I—let the clutter move into my heart that made me so judgmental of others. It was an acquired flaw, because kids weren't born with it.

Chapter 15
Money and Failed Attempts at Entrepreneurship

Money is important. From what I can tell, it always has been. I first realized its importance when, at about age five, I rode my tricycle four blocks to Hartley's neighborhood grocery store to treat myself to ice cream, candy or a Nehi orange soda. I must have woke up stupid that day, because the need for "serious" money for any of these items had not crossed my mind. I had two pennies and, to my way of thinking, that should have been enough to buy about anything I craved. After browsing for a while, I decided to buy a Dreamsicle, an orange-and-vanilla ice cream bar on a stick. I confidently took my purchase to the counter and asked Mr. Hartley how much he needed. When he told me ten cents, I about messed in my britches. I told him I had changed my mind about the Dreamsicle and was going to look around some more. One at a time, I took several candy bars and a Nehi strawberry soda (they were out of orange) to the counter and asked, "How much?" Everything I asked about was at least a nickel. I was getting pretty bummed out, and Mr. Hartley was getting tired of playing the 'how much" game. Finally, he asked me how much money I had. I showed him two pennies and he nodded and started showing me just what I could buy with my timid fortune. Basically, I could buy two pieces of bubble gum, one large jawbreaker, two small peanut butter logs, or one piece of bubble gum and one peanut butter log. I opted for two peanut butter logs. I took my trike and my candy behind Hartley's, sat under a shady elm and slowly savored the two small, sticky candy bars. They were good, but they weren't nearly as good as that Dreamsicle would have been. Then and there, I decided I needed to devote some serious time to improving my economic lot in life. From that day through the sixth grade, I didn't make a lot of money, but trying to do so led me down some interesting paths.

One day soon after my failed attempt to buy a Dreamsicle, I rode my tricycle five blocks from home to the east side of South Washington Street in search of adventure. As I rode past the Snider's house, I noticed a bunch of interesting items lying on the ground under their two large magnolia trees. They were shaped like hand grenades and even had rough, somewhat patterned exteriors that looked like the exteriors of the neutered grenades that many soldiers brought back from the War as souvenirs. I was in the dark as to what these "grenades" really were, but I knew their appearance, size and their feel would make them wildly popular with all my friends as we played war in the vacant lot near our house. The more I thought about it, the more I realized what an incredible "find" I had happened upon. I jumped on my trike and peddled as fast as I could toward home. I had a plan. When I got back home, I tied my red wagon onto the back of my trike and raced back to the Snider's house and my newfound gold mine. Though out of breath from the ten blocks of high-speed pedaling, I hurriedly loaded all the "grenades" in my wagon and headed for home. I must have had thirty to forty of the "grenades" in my Radio Flyer wagon, and the feeling of power that raced through my veins was pretty heady stuff.

My friend, David Reeves, lived about midway between the Snider's house and my house. I spotted David swinging in his backyard and decided it was time to put my "plan" into action. I yelled for him to come and look at the "hand grenades" I had found. David ambled over, trying to not look too interested. When he saw the "grenades" in my wagon, his wariness took a hike and he begged me to let him hold one. After I explained to him how much fun we could have throwing these "grenades" at the enemy, he was hooked. When he asked me if he could have some of them, I told him they were far too valuable to give away but that he could buy a couple if he wanted to at a nickel apiece. He asked me to wait while he went in his house to see if he could find some money. After about fifteen minutes, David came out of his house with a brown paper sack. He told me he couldn't find any money, but he would give me all the pirate's treasure in the brown bag in exchange for the "grenades." I dumped the contents of the bag onto the sidewalk that ran beside his house and was blown away by the beautiful jewelry that spilled out. There were rings, watches, necklaces, pins, earrings and other stuff, too. I loaded it all back in the brown bag, and told him, "It's a deal." We unloaded my wagon and I, along with my treasure, headed home. This five-year-old entrepreneur had just swung his first major "deal" and was well on the road to great wealth!

I crawled onto my bed and emptied the bag onto the bedspread. I then sorted it, admired it and tried to figure out how I could convert it to cash. After concluding that it wasn't enough "stuff" to stock a new jewelry store, I decided I would either have to sell it door-to-door or open a jewelry stand on a busy street corner. I figured if you could sell lemonade from a corner stand, you could easily sell fine jewelry. I wrestled with my marketing plan through supper and was nearing some decisions when my entrepreneurial dreams were shattered by a phone call. It seems David's mother called my mother and told her David had given me all of her jewelry in exchange for some "things" that later turned out to be magnolia tree seed pods. Phooey. Mother carefully put the jewelry back into the brown paper bag and the two of us walked to the Reeves's house to return it to Mrs. Reeves. The two mothers laughed at the deal I had structured with David. I guess they thought it was "cute." I thought the whole episode sucked, and I didn't find it funny at all. The next day, I retrieved all my "grenades." They lay under the mimosa tree in our backyard until they rotted. Rats.

Most all my adventures and misadventures involved my best friend, Terry. Despite occasional spats and fights, we were pretty much inseparable. Terry lived across the street from me and the path from my front door to his back door—through Dickie Cole's back yard—was well-worn. It was only natural that most of my money-making schemes were really the end product of two great minds working together—mine and Terry's. In truth, Terry wasn't very good at coming up with money-making schemes, but he was always willing to "partner" on any venture I conjured up.

Terry's family had a small farm out on Fern Lake Cutoff, about six or seven miles from our homes. It was part of his Dad's parents' homestead and two of Terry's aunts owned the acreages on either side of his dad's land. Terry's Aunt Mae and Uncle Cecil lived on their acreage and had a small garden, but none of the three owners actively farmed their land. There were a few cows on his Aunt Iris's place, but not enough to ruin the raw-land look and feel of the farm. That meant that when Terry and I spent the day at Aunt Mae's—which we occasionally did—we had free run of about 150 acres of woods. We built hideouts, dug holes, climbed trees, sat on logs, and just generally turned our imaginations loose. Now that I think back, I'm not sure we had as much freedom in the woods as we thought we did. I seem to recall Uncle Cecil just "happening by" on more than one occasion. I'm almost positive he didn't have a moonshine still on the land, so he had no reason to be in the woods other than to be checking up on us. The farm came into play on a couple of our first "partnership" ventures.

The first money-making scheme Terry and I co-imagined happened when the new Montgomery Ward catalogue arrived in Terry's mail. Terry and I snared it from his dining room table and took it to his front porch for some serious perusing. We were chiefly interested in two sections—women's lingerie and toys—but we went through the entire big, thick catalogue one page at a time. Nothing much captured our attention until we came to a section dedicated to beekeeping. The section portrayed beekeeping as an easy way to make extra money. All one had to do was to set up some hives, put some bees in them, wait until they made honey, then harvest the honey, bottle it and sell it for big bucks. For some reason, it sounded doable to us, so we began constructing our business plan. The plan consisted of buying all the beekeeping items Montgomery Ward offered and setting up operations on Terry's farm. We skimmed right over our three biggest problems—money to buy the equipment, what to do with the equipment if/when we got it and how we would get to and from the farm to do the work. We were only eight, so lines of credit, technical know-how and driver's licenses were not among our corporate assets. Rather than deal with those issues, we chose to focus on what we would do with all the money we would make as honey barons.

Terry's Aunt Mae was the manager of the local Montgomery Ward catalogue store, so we thought the first thing we should do would be to ride our bikes to her store and get her to tell us how much money we needed to buy everything required to get us up and running. We also needed to know when we would need to pay. Did we have to pay for everything up front, or could we pay from the profits that were sure to roll in? Aunt Mae took the pencil from its perch on top of her ear and began to write down our "order" on a blank order form. It must have been a slow day at Montgomery Ward, because she treated us like we were real important customers. The list of goods we wanted was quite long, and when she finished it and totaled its costs, she pushed her glasses up on her forehead and told us it would cost us $238.50 to be commercial apiarists. She went on to tell us we had to pay the bill before the order could be placed. We thanked her, took the order form, and folded it up; I crammed it into my jeans pocket. The bike ride back home was a long, tough trek. We were greatly discouraged, but we felt like one or both of our dads would see our great potential and loan us the needed start-up capital. Wrong. Each dad, in turn, did a fair job of listening to our enthusiastic appeal for backing, and said, "No." Neither elaborated on their reasoning or professed admiration for our initiative. They just said, "No." So much for the honey business.

Our next "big deal" also involved the Weeks's farm, Aunt Mae and Uncle Cecil. Terry and I had spent a Friday night with them, and when we woke up Saturday morning, we were ready for some outside adventure. Aunt Mae made us breakfast and served us some fresh sassafras tea with it. For you folks who may not know what sassafras is, it's a tree/bush that grows wild in East Texas, and, when boiled, its roots yield a fragrant extract that makes a root beer–flavored tea. It was good. We were told sassafras flavoring led to the invention of root beer, so when Uncle Cecil told us he dug up the roots right there on the farm, I started seeing potential dollar signs. Terry and I quickly huddled and decided our future wealth would come from the digging and selling of sassafras roots. We talked Uncle Cecil into showing us where to find the roots and how to harvest them. After a fifteen-minute lesson, Uncle Cecil left to re-stain his picnic table and Terry and I were left to harvest on our own.

Terry and I dug and cut roots the rest of the day and then hauled our sizeable yield back to the house. We were near giddy with our success. We spread our roots out on the back-porch floor and stood by as we saw Uncle Cecil heading our way. He took in our smiles of pride and complimented us on our hard work. He then bent down and started sniffing and examining each root. After giving them the smell test, he started dividing our crop into two piles. When he finished sorting the roots, we noticed the pile on his right was much, much bigger than the pile on his left. When we asked about why there were two piles, he told us that the small pile on his left was of sassafras roots, and that, unfortunately, all of the roots in the big pile on his right were not sassafras, but were, in fact, roots from young sweet gum trees. He went on to tell us that no one on God's green earth would drink sweet gum tea as it would pucker you up tighter than Aunt Tillie's purse strings. Day wasted, and another business failure for Eubanks & Weeks, Inc. If a fellow wants to make his fortune in the sassafras business, he'd best be able to tell the difference between sassafras roots and sweet gum roots. Terry and I couldn't.

Across the road from the farm stood a fairly large pond that at night came alive with the sounds of crickets and deep-throated bullfrogs. After Terry and I learned that people loved to eat frog legs, guess what? Yep, we launched our frog-legs-for-profit venture. That night, armed with one frog gig, a strong flash light and two wooden paddles—all provided by Uncle Cecil—we crawled through the barbed wire fence that bordered the pond and went straight to the aluminum boat that stayed pulled up on the pond's bank. We turned the boat over on its side to drain the accumulated rain water, righted it, loaded our gear into it and shoved off to look for frogs. At this point, I should briefly describe the inner workings of just what successful frog gigging entails.

Frogs hang around the edge of bodies of water at night and bellow. The deeper the bellow, the bigger the bullfrog. Those hunting them are armed with a long pole with a metal thing attached to the end of it that has two or three sharp, barbed tines on it. That's the gig. The gigger sneaks up to within the length of the pole, freezes the frog with a bright light and thrusts the gig into the frog. You then throw the frog into your burlap tote sack and move on down to the next croaker. That's how frog gigging works, or that's how it's supposed to work. Terry and I decided he would paddle the boat, and I would operate the light with my left hand and the gig with my right. We were doomed from the start. Terry kept hitting the aluminum boat with the paddle, and I kept telling him to quit making so much noise. Soon, Terry and I were arguing at full throttle about who was making the most noise. It was a moot point, as all the frogs went mute and hid out. I think they all probably shared a good giggle at our expense. Another entrepreneurial failure. We turned out to be frog frighteners, not frog giggers. Drat.

Not all my money-making efforts involved Terry. One involved my friend Billy Worley, who was three years older than me. Billy's mother worked for the primo liberal law firm in Marshall. It was the Jones, Jones and Jones Law Firm, and it was very, very successful. It was also very active in local, state and national politics. When a young Republican named George H. W. Bush challenged the incumbent Democrat Ralph Yarborough for his Senate seat, Jones, Jones and Jones hired Billy to walk all over Marshall putting pro-Yarborough campaign fliers under every car's windshield wiper. Billy had their permission to hire a friend to help him. He hired me. We loaded boxes full of fliers and set about our mission. We walked and walked and distributed lots of Yarborough fliers. Boy it was hot, and those boxes got to feeling awful heavy. To rest, we sat under an oak tree on West Burleson Street that Sam Houston had spoken beneath early in Texas's history. Now, before I tell you the rest of the story, you need to understand that Billy was not an enthusiastic worker. In fact, I feel safe in saying he was hard-work averse. While resting under the tree, Billy spotted the storm drain on the other side of the street. After a brief pause, he gathered up the remaining fliers, walked across the street and dumped them down the drain. He had just cut our workload by probably 70 percent. We then walked over to Abraham's Grocery and drank two Nehi sodas each. After killing what Billy said was enough time, we went back to Jones, Jones and Jones, reported that we had completed our work and collected $6.50 each. I liked working for Billy, but I would never hire him. In spite of our dismal performance, Yarborough won the election. Many years later, when Mr. Bush was Vice President of the United States, I had the occasion to tell him this story of Billy's and my perverted effort to help him beat Yarborough. He seemed to enjoy the story. And I can tell you, that after meeting him and seeing what a gentleman he was, I wish Billy and I had thrown all of the Yarborough fliers away.

The only time I remember Daddy paying me for a chore around the house was when he paid me five cents for every caterpillar I pulled off his many rose bushes one week he was away on business. When Daddy got home and counted the caterpillars I had put in the glass jar during his absence, my take came to something like a dollar fifty. I guess that was more than he had anticipated, because he paid me, told me I had done a good job, and then fired me. I tried to expand the market for my caterpillar-picking business by taking an empty jar and going to all of the houses in the neighborhood that had rose bushes and offering my services. Mrs. Allen, who lived down on Medill Street, was the only one who hired me. I only found four caterpillars munching her rose leaves, but she gave me a quarter anyway. I decided there was little ongoing demand for caterpillar removal so I shuttered this new venture.

I guess this is as good of a time as ever to tell about one of my brother Homer's money adventures. It seems that when he was just a wee fellow, someone gave him a nickel and, trying to teach him our nation's monetary system, explained that there were five pennies in a nickel. Homer was puzzled by this story and set about finding the five pennies that were hiding in his nickel. He took Daddy's hammer to the sidewalk in front of our house and commenced beating the puddin' out of the nickel trying to free the pennies that were inside. Finally, he gave up and took the near-destroyed nickel in to Mother, where he told her his nickel was no good because there weren't five pennies in it. Money has always made folks do wild, crazy and stupid things. By the way, we still have that fractured nickel.

Once when I was over at Tuck's house playing, we decided to go looking for empty soda bottles, each of which had a three-cent redemption value. After a couple of hours of digging through trash piles and ditches, we had accumulated about twelve to fifteen bottles and decided it was time to go to Min-A-Pak, a predecessor of 7-Eleven I mentioned before, and cash in. Mr. Skaggs, the owner, paid us our money, which we promptly spent on candy or sodas. We were outside enjoying the rewards of our scavenging when Mr. Skaggs came out of the store carrying the bottles we had just redeemed. We watched as he took them behind the store and put them in a wood-frame bin that was covered in chicken wire. He had scads of bottles in the bin, and Tuck and I noticed it wasn't locked. A plan quickly formed. Yep, we rode around the block three or four times, stowed our bikes, crept up behind Min-A-Pak and liberated eight bottles from their chicken-wire prison. We promptly took them into the store for our twenty-four cents and bought baseball cards. We pulled this heist one more time and decided we'd better quit while we were ahead. Besides, we were both suffering from guilt instilled by our Baptist upbringings. We went back to Tuck's and played catch.

By the time I was ten, I made most of my money doing things like mowing the neighbor's lawn, washing the occasional car, selling Christmas cards door-to-door or, maybe, raking someone's autumn yard. In the summer, I played organized baseball every year until I made the high school team. Most of the games were played at City Park, where there was one field for Little Leaguers and another for the older kids. The municipal swimming pool, a separate wading pool, four tennis courts, swings and a miniature golf course completed the scene at the park. The park was a beehive of activity Monday through Saturday nights. The Lions Club ran the concession stands that served the park, and, at age ten, I got me a job working in the main stand. It was run by a man named J.B., who drove the delivery truck for a printing firm in Marshall during the day. I worked side-by-side with J.B. before and after my games and on nights when I didn't play ball. J.B. had two big hearing aids and a speech impediment that made him almost impossible to understand. We got along great, perhaps, because for some unknown reason, I could understand him and I spoke loud enough for him to hear me. I also knew how to make change. He paid me seventy-five cents an hour and one free snow cone at the end of work each night. After closing, I'd walk the ten blocks home and show-up with money in my pocket and a red ring around my mouth from my strawberry snow cone. Interestingly enough, the seventy-five cents an hour was the most I made per hour until I hooked on with a highway construction job when I was sixteen.

One time an avid rock collector brought his collection to Miss Badget's sixth-grade class, spread the specimens out on tables and told us about them. I thoroughly enjoyed looking at them all and learning about them. I was particularly enthralled when he showed us some clay marbles that he said had belonged to members of the Caddo Indian tribe more than one hundred years ago. All of us boys seemed to focus on these marbles at the expense of the mica, feldspar, obsidian and granite. When I noticed their fascination with the clay marbles, I hatched a money-making scheme. I decided I would dig up some clay, make marbles from it, bake them, and sell them as Caddo Indian marbles for a quarter each. When my first batch was "cured" I took them to the outer reaches of my neighborhood and tried to peddle them. I sold two to Ronnie Ford and three to Richard Primo. My success was short-lived. The next afternoon, Ronnie and Richard showed up at my house demanding a refund. Apparently, the Indian marbles finished drying out overnight and split open. I refunded their money and restored peace and harmony in the 'hood.

When I was in the sixth grade, I always ate lunch in the cafeteria. The meal cost a quarter and a carton of milk was a dime. I had no gripe with the quality of food, just the quantity. They never gave me enough to fill me up. I could have eaten twenty fish sticks but they only put two on my plate. They gave me one puny little pork chop when I could've eaten five. You get the picture. It broke my heart when I would take my totally empty plate to the window for dirty dishes and I would see kids turning in plates that had hardly been touched. How could they? I'm starving and they are throwing their food away! It went on like this for the first two or three weeks of school, and then one day, our principal, Mr. Murphy, came into our class and asked if anyone would like to volunteer to work in the cafeteria each day at lunch. The pay was a free lunch. I threw my hand up so fast I almost dislocated my shoulder. When I reported to my job the next day, I was told I would work in the return window. My job would be to take all plates, dump any uneaten food into the big, gray plastic barrel and load the dirty dishes into a wire rack that fit into the washing machine. I had died and gone to heaven. I ate all the uneaten food off my classmates' plates I wanted. I had to be the happiest cafeteria worker in America from that day forward. Full—full at last.

Finding money someone else had lost was always a major contributor to my personal war on poverty. I was good at spotting lost pennies, nickels, dimes and quarters. But, honestly, I found a whole lot more pennies than I did quarters. No doubt I was adept at knowing where to look for lost coins; (i.e., under the monkey bars on the playground, under the ledge at the base of the concession stand at the Paramount or Lynn Theater, in the cracks between the cushions on the sofas in the Paramount's lobby, under the pew cushions at church, under the bleachers at the local ball parks and in the changing cubicles at Sears, Penney's, Wiseman's and Beall's in downtown Marshall.) While I did okay, Andy Maxwell and his cousin, Lacy, blew my mind when they told me how much they "made" taking tip money off the tables in New

York when they accompanied their mothers on a visit to the city. I thought about applying their tactics in the cafes, coffee shops and restaurants in Marshall, but I knew all the waitresses and their families I would be taking the tip money from, and just couldn't do it. They needed the money worse than I did.

Back in the '50s, there were only three or four families in Marshall who had a swimming pool in their yard, and none of them opened their pools to the public. Therefore, we commoners had to go to the city pool, which was in our main city park. Each clear summer day, kids would line up in front of the pool entrance by the dozens eagerly waiting for this heavenly hole in the ground to open. First, we had to pay our dime. Next, we were herded into the showers—girls to the left, boys to the right—for the coldest rinse-off imaginable. We were then inspected to make certain we hadn't tried to skip the shower bit. They were very serious about keeping cooties and dirt out of our city pool. Sometimes the smell of chlorine was so strong one could hardly breathe. My brother, Homer, told me they put so much chlorine in the water to neutralize all the pee that swimmers added to the pool's water. Lastly, we were given a wire basket in which we stored our clothes, billfolds, shoes, towels, etc. When all these rituals had been observed, we could enter the pool area. Lord, it was great!

Once in the pool, my buds and I—Terry, Charlie, Frank, Wist and Clarence, or some combination of us—always played a game we came up with called "The Creature from the Black Lagoon," which was loosely based on the B-horror-movie by the same name. The rules were fuzzy then, and now they seem even fuzzier. Basically, as I recall, one of us was dubbed the creature and all the others tried to avoid contact with the monster. If mauled by the creature, the maulee became the creature and the whole drama was repeated. Dumb game, but it kept us occupied for hours.

Terrorizing each other playing "creature" caused us to exert a whole lot of energy, which, in turn, made us terribly hungry. That hunger became tortuous when Mrs. Annette Hightower, the lady who ran the snack bar, put hamburger patties on the grill. The aromas that came off that grill were all-consuming and downright ruthless. The hamburgers sold for a quarter, and Mother always sent me to the pool with twenty cents—ten cents for admission and ten cents for a soda or candy bar. What was a starving boy to do? Well, this boy stopped playing "creature," adjusted his goggles, and began a meticulous search of the pool's bottom for loose change that may have fallen from someone's swimsuit. That search usually paid dividends on two fronts.

First of all, I nearly always found enough money to enable me to buy a hamburger, and, secondly, I got to enjoy the sight of all the girls' legs. The older I got, the value of the second benefit began to outpace the value of the first. In retrospect, I received a third benefit from my goggled underwater exploration. I received a head start on my sex education by just observing what young couples did to each other underwater when they didn't notice a kid swimming by.

The biggest find of money that I didn't have to return occurred on a Saturday morning when Terry and I decided we wanted to go to the Kiddie Show at the Paramount. Terry's mother gave him enough money for his ticket and some goodies, but I was dead broke and Mother was at work and Daddy was having the oil changed on his '54 Chevy Bel Air at Moseley's Phillips 66 gas station. Mother gave me the okay to go to the movie, but she said I'd have to wait for Daddy to get home for my money. Time was short so I couldn't wait for Daddy to get home. I told Terry we should start our walk to the Paramount. He thought this long walk would turn out to be a wasted effort since I had zero money. I told him not to worry because I would find enough money on the way to downtown. He started rapid eye blinking, which symbolized his skepticism. But, for some reason, I had a solid belief I really would find enough money. I had no doubt—none. We had finished about three-quarters of our trek and I was still penniless despite having walked two miles with my head and eyes locked in the down position. As we passed in front of the Central Baptist Church, I noticed a glint coming from the grass in front of the church. When I checked it out, I found not one, but three shiny fifty-cent pieces—one dollar and fifty-cents! Terry was amazed, and I was relieved. Since that day, I have believed in the power of faith and confidence, and, may I add, it wasn't lost on me that my treasure was revealed to me in front of a church. Hmmmmm.

I had one more source of "found" money I should reveal. Whenever I went downtown, I always stopped by to visit Mr. Stacy, one of two cobblers in Marshall. He and Mrs. Stacy had been friends of my family for a couple of generations. Each time I visited him, he gave me a nickel or dime as I was leaving. He also scruffed my hair as he said goodbye. That was okay with me because I had a burr cut and nothing got mussed up. When I left his shop with the wonderful smell of leather in me and on me, I next went to see Mrs. Stacy, who was the cosmetologist at Wiseman's Department Store. It was a two-block trip. Mrs. Stacy always hugged me and she always smelled so good. Mother told me Mrs. Stacy wore Charles of the Ritz. I didn't know who Charles was, but I sure liked the smell of his "Ritz" stuff. While they were physically only a couple of blocks away from each other, their smells were miles apart: both great, but miles apart. Mrs. Stacy, like her husband, always gave me a nickel or dime, too. I didn't go see them to get their money. I visited them because they were "family' and I loved them. By the way, their first names were Crant and Ress. Different, huh?

Unless a child grows up and inherits big bucks, hits the lottery or marries wealth, that child will be compelled to spend a good part of his life in pursuit of money. It's called a job, and we stay at it because we never outgrow the desire to move up from a candy bar to a hamburger. Need creates energy, enthusiasm and creativity. I'm glad the silver spoon never touched my lips, because I've had a lot of great adventures trying to come up with enough money to buy one of Mrs. Hightower's hamburgers.

There were many more stories about my search for money, but, suffice it to say, I hustled. While I usually managed to keep a little spending money in my pockets, believe me, there were plenty of times when all I had in my pockets was lint. That pattern still holds.

Chapter 16
Things to Do with Grass, Weeds, Flowers, and Fruit

Normally, I would get five or six toys and a few new pieces of clothing for Christmas each year. I would get a couple more toys and maybe some new underwear and socks on my birthday in April. I always figured I was one of Santa's favorite kids since I got so many gifts. I was absolutely overcome with joy when I first peeped into the living room and spotted the pile of presents under our tree each Christmas morning. Today, lots of kids get more toys when they accompany their parents on a Saturday trip to Target for towels and fertilizer than we did at Christmas, but they couldn't come close to the all-consuming joy we felt those Christmas mornings. Each year, Terry, Charlie, Clarence and I would gang up after the unwrapping of the gifts in our respective homes and make the rounds to each of our houses to see what Santa had left us.

Playing soon ensued at a feverish pitch. Over time, the new wore off our toys, and we were generally bored with them by April or May. Kids today are usually bored by Sunday with the new goodies they got on Saturday. When we reached the point of being bored with our toys, it was time to crank up our imaginations and explore the creative highway. At least that's what we did in the 1950s. Today's bored kids seem to fight their boredom by hopping on the electronic highway. Whatever works.

When I recall the many places my imagination and creativity took me, and how much fun I had on the journeys, the memories are too many to corral. There were times I just sat under a shade tree and thought about exotic places, sports stardom or pretty girls (I still think about one of those). However, there were times when I needed action, not fantasies. That's when, in a most utilitarian fashion, I started doing things with grass, weeds, flowers and fruit—all of which were in abundance in my neighborhood. Let me share with you some of the things my buddies and I did with those no-cost materials that helped us pass countless hours when we couldn't think of anything else to do.

Grass and Weeds: Good stands of grass—particularly St. Augustine grass—always yielded blades that when stretched tautly between your two thumbs held together and pointed upward could be turned into a multitonal whistle when blown on. A gifted grass blower could play a melody on his blade and entertain the girls at recess. I remember one time when I was in the second grade, I held Lynn Abney, Joan Bergstrom, and Patti Dickerson spellbound for an entire recess period by giving them a grass blade concert, during which I "blew" about all of the tunes I could think of. As I recall, I knocked their socks off with my version of "When the Saints Go Marchin' In." I concluded they knew talent when they saw or heard it. Lynn and I went steady for two weeks after my performance. I was good at blade blowing; Terry, not so much. On the other hand, I spent countless hours looking through clover patches trying to find a four-leaf specimen. They were supposed to be good luck. I never found one. Terry found a bunch of them.

Whenever we found dandelions, we plucked them and blew their spores off just to watch the breeze toy with them. Today, I realize we were actually infesting our neighborhood with dandelions by dispersing their spores. Blowing on dandelions wasn't much fun, so if I had known I was just helping them multiply, I would have gone back to playing lilts on my grass blade.

Most of the yards in my neighborhood were covered with Bermuda grass, which apparently was the perfect host grass for not only dandelions, but for stickers and cockleburs as well. If stickers and cockleburs were animals, they would be on a par with scorpions and fire ants, because they made going barefooted a miserable and painful exercise. If one stepped on a dried clump of stickers, it was like stepping on a wasp nest. If you did step on a sticker patch, you had to spend the next fifteen minutes pulling the little devils out of your feet one at a time. Cockleburs were spiny little balls of needle-like stickers perched on four-to-five-inch stems that rose above the ground. They were to be steered away from, unless, of course, you were in a cocklebur war. You see, you could break the stem off at the ground, and while holding on to it, hurl it at whoever you were warring with. The head of the bur would stick firmly to your enemy's clothing. Shirt shots were the most effective because the stickers would penetrate the cotton T-shirts we all wore and cause your buddy to grimace as he gingerly removed the bur from his torso. Rules of war dictated that head shots were forbidden. Dickey Brassell usually broke our version of the Geneva Convention by throwing for the head of his adversary.

When I was in the country or down at Caddo Lake visiting with Aunt Bon and Uncle Curly, I could always find bitterweed, a kind of ragweed, to break off and chew on. The bitter-weed earned its name because it was very bitter and overloaded with pucker power. It brought tears to my eyes. Other than those three problems, it was pretty good. Sounds like fun, huh? I'm not sure why chewing on bitterweed was the thing to do, but *everybody* did it. Chewing on a stalk of bitterweed was something you only did when you were with your friends. If you were alone, you'd never put that crappy stuff in your mouth.

Flowers: One plant that everybody liked was honeysuckle. It grew wild in East Texas and lots of folks had it in their yards. I'm not going to waste time telling folks how to extract honey from a honeysuckle bloom, because I'm betting everyone has done it. If you haven't, well, get a life. Like I said, everyone likes nature's sweet nectar, me included. However, I must tell you it takes a long, long time to coax enough honey from these honeysuckle blooms to feel like you've had dessert. After years of sucking honey from the honeysuckle, I have no problem understanding why bees, butterflies and humming birds are so small. It just takes too long to suck down enough honey to add any bulk. Honeysuckle juice was never a threat to replace popsicles or Nehi sodas on this little boy's wish list.

Flowers could be fun, too. For example, curl your index finger around so the end of it touches the inside of the end of your thumb. If you did it correctly, you now have a circle or hole going down through your palm and remaining fingers. Next, place a nice, big rose petal across the hole and hit it hard with the palm of your free hand. A good petal popper could scare his neighbor's dog with the loud pop he ignited with just one rose petal. A bored boy could pluck and pop enough petals in one sitting to denude his mother's favorite American Beauty in no time.

Another thing to do with flowers was to pick one (or more) of any variety and present it to any female you wanted to make happy. The presentation of a flower or small bouquet to a mother, a teacher, a girlfriend or a future girlfriend always brought a sigh, a smile and a sugar-coated "thank you." It worked that way on women in the 1950s, and it will work on women in the 3050s. Would a man wear a corsage? No. But a woman would not only proudly wear a corsage, but also would press it in a book and save it for years. My life-long friend Susie Musser Galik confessed to me just a year or two ago that she envied my sixth-grade girlfriend, Carol Marshall, the entire time we "dated." She didn't envy Carol because she "had" me; she envied Carol because she got to wear camellia corsages handmade by my mother to all our dances. Women and flowers have a thing going that most of us fellows underappreciate. I've often thought a politician could save all of his campaign advertising budget and win the female vote just by giving each one a rose.

Continuing on the "fun with flowers" theme, I'll bet most all of us have held a daisy or sunflower and plucked its petals off one at a time saying, "she loves me, she loves me not," just hoping the last petal he plucks is on "she loves me." See, there are lots of things to do with flowers, particularly if you like girls.

Fruits and Berries: When I was a kid, about all I could think of doing with fruits or berries was to eat them, throw them or try to make wine with them. As hungry as I always was, there was a limit to how many pears I could eat in one sitting, and pears were about the only fruit grown in our neighborhood. We had three very productive pear trees, and the Paces had

two that had to be record-setting pear producers. I loved our
pears, but it was always more fun to steal a pear or two from
the Pace's trees for some reason. The Paces would have been
tickled pink to give me however many pears I wanted, but it
was more fun to steal them. I hope that's not a window into
my character. When my friends and I were tired of pears, but
were still feeling "fruity," we would ride our bikes about three
blocks west of my house to either a vacant lot behind Richard
Magrill's house or to a small section of woods behind Wiley
College, two spots where blackberries and plums grew wild.
There were persimmon trees there, too, but nobody messed
with them. When ripe, persimmons were uncontrollably
messy. Possums, wasps and bees loved them. A human had
to be mighty hungry to choke down a persimmon. When it
came to blackberries and plums, we would eat them as soon
as we found them so the only part of the berries or plums
that made it home with us was the berry juice that stained
our shirts, jeans and fingernails.

In 1957, our two fifth-grade classes worked together on
preparing part of the decorations for our school's Thanksgiving
assembly. We were to cover the bottoms of a bunch of aluminum pie plates with fresh cranberries. We dutifully glued
the cranberries in place, and took them to the cafeteria and
placed one on each table that had been set up for the assembly
program. When we returned to our classrooms, Mrs. Brown
and Miss Undean told us to take the big bucket of unused

cranberries out to the garbage cans behind the cafeteria. Frank Timmins, Charlie Starke and John Mark Phillips had been given the disposal assignment, but before they even made it out the door, Frank grabbed a handful of the juicy berries and started pelting Charlie and John Mark. Charlie and John Mark returned fire, and as the berry war spilled out onto the school ground, lots of other kids bailed out of their classrooms and got into the free-for-all. Cranberries were flying in all directions and the battle went on until all the berries had been thrown. What made the cranberry war so bad was that everyone had on white shirts with a red crepe paper bandana around their neck because we were to sing at the Thanksgiving assembly program. Frank, Charlie, John Mark, Sally Van Wert, Kathy Dossett and at least ten other classmates had big, honking-red cranberry stains on their white shirts. It was a mess. Our two classes were marched into Mrs. Brown's classroom and given a tearful butt-chewing because of our irresponsible behavior and the fact that we had ruined the school's big Thanksgiving shindig. Who would have thought that one bucket of cranberries could get fifty kids in so much trouble?

My brothers were ten and thirteen years older than me, and as teenagers, they were always flirting with impropriety—particularly Robert. He was the one who was ten years my senior. One time when he was about fifteen or sixteen, he and one of his friends, "Pinky" Hughes, decided to make wine. They were very secretive about the process they were employing, so I only picked up a few of the steps. I knew they ground up some kind of fruit until it was juice, added water to it, sealed it up in a jar and put it away to "age." I didn't know what, if anything, else they added or whether "aging" took twenty minutes or twenty years. Even with our limited knowledge, Terry and I decided that if Robert and "Pinky" could make wine, we could make wine. We found an old Mason jar, took one of Mother's pans for grinding up our fruit, pilfered Daddy's hammer for use as a grinding tool and set about our mission. Since berries and plums were out of season and we had overdosed on pears, we selected chinaberries as our fruit. At this point, I should tell you chinaberries are round, grow on trees and, when ripe are vile-smelling-and-tasting yellow berries. About the only thing they were good for was as ammo for shooting in a slingshot when they were green and hard. Even today, I suspect they are poisonous, because birds won't eat them. I don't know what possessed us to use chinaberries, but I guess we were in a hurry and they were both handy and abundant. After squashing them with our hammer, we filled half of our jar with chinaberry juice. It looked like vomit, and it smelled worse than it looked. We decided the addition of some red berries from our nandina bush would, at least, make it look better. We added some water and stuck the jar under our house for "aging." We decided making wine was easy, but we weren't stupid. We knew better than to drink our wine, even after it was "aged." We decided that once it was ready, we would put it in a bowl and watch the birds, dogs and cats drink it and get drunk. What fun! An hour or so later, we pronounced it ready and filled Belle's water bowl with the "wine." We hid behind a camellia bush and eagerly waited for birds or beasts to gobble it up and stagger around drunk. It didn't happen. Mogen David wine didn't have to worry about us as competition. Our wine-making days were over. I still don't know if Robert's and "Pinkie's" concoction made wine or not.

Doing things with grass, weeds, flowers and fruit required active imaginations. Me and my friends came close to over-working ours. While I have enjoyed recounting some of the things we did with those items, I must confess something. I never figured out what to do with pine straw or pine sap, and it always bothered me. Both looked good, smelled good and felt good; but it stumped me completely as to what they were good for. I made beds out of pine straw, but it wasn't that comfortable, and I got ticks from it. I used it to start fires, but not many. Besides, arson was frowned on. I tried chewing the sap, but it tasted horrible and stuck to your teeth. Any ideas?

Chapter 17
Belle, Dot, and Stubby

My neighborhood, like most of those in America in the early 1950s, was bursting with freedom. I guess we were all on a post-war high. There were very few fences and all of us kids had free rein until dark to explore the neighborhood in search of fun and adventure. Also, there were no leash laws so our dogs enjoyed the same freedom of movement we did.

Our family dog was a beautiful black-and-tan hound with a bit of bluetick coonhound thrown in. Her name was Belle. She was really brother Robert's dog, but because I was younger and didn't have as many social and school obligations, I spent more time with her. He went off to Texas A&M when I was just eight. A local prominent coon hunter named "Skillet" Fisher had given Belle to Robert because she was the runt of a new litter of pups from his prized coonhound, and her legs were so badly bowed he figured she'd never be able to stand, much less run with the other coonhounds and,

Belle watching for Dot

thus, he wouldn't be able sell her or hunt with her. Robert often hunted with the Fishers because "Skillet's" son, Dick, was one of his best friends. Also, knowing my brother was a good boy probably influenced Mr. Fisher's gift of the little puppy to him. All that said, when it came to "salvaging" the puny pup, it seems Mr. Fisher underestimated both Belle and brother Robert. Robert put Belle's tiny bent legs in some splints he made from Popsicle sticks and hand-fed the helpless little pup for weeks from an eyedropper. At first, Belle could only stand when propped up, falling each time she tried to walk. Mother and Daddy didn't think Belle would make it, but they, like Skillet Fisher, underestimated Belle and my patient and determined brother. Before long, Belle got to where she could walk a bit, then lope, and finally, to where she could run like the wind—all on perfectly straight legs. She grew up to be a graceful, majestic animal with a voice that could fill Sabine River Bottom with a sound that thrilled coon hunters for miles around.

Good coonhounds needed to have six major qualities:

1. speed, which enabled them to keep up with the coon during the hunt;

2. agility, which was needed to pick their way through briars and thick underbrush during the chase;

3. a good nose, necessary for staying on scent during the chase;

4. stamina, because a coon hunt and chase could go on for miles and miles;

5. a loud, clear voice, so the hunters could pursue the chase by listening to the hounds as they raced through the woods; and,

6. courage, because sometimes the coon got tired of running and decided to stop and fight.

Belle got high marks on all six counts. Robert took her hunting with Skillet a number of times and she was a star. Skillet tried many times to buy her from Robert, but my brother would have sold me before he would have sold Belle. Robert and Belle shared an unwavering loyalty to each other. When Robert went off to college in 1955, Belle's hunting days were over and she retired to the yard. While Belle loved me, her heart clearly belonged to Robert, as well it should have. He saved her life with love and care and patience. Belle rewarded his good deed with a love bond she reserved for him.

Before Belle joined our family, we somehow ended up with a Chow named Chuck for a short time. I was too young to know how we got Chuck, but I wasn't too young to understand that Chuck hated everyone and didn't want to be touched or played with. Daddy kept Chuck chained up to the pin oak in our backyard. All of us knew exactly how far Chuck could stretch that chain, and we stayed well out of striking range. When anyone fed Chuck, that person used a garden rake to reach inside the danger zone, hook onto the feeding bowl's edge and pull it outside the reach of the chain. When the bowl was filled, the rake operator pushed the bowl back within Chuck's territory. Daddy was the only one who could enter the danger zone, and his ability to do so followed an intense stare-down between Chuck and Dad. Having been the recipients of some of Daddy's stare-downs, my two brothers and I understood Chuck's cowering from him. Chuck wasn't a pet. He was a resident monster we threw meat to once a day. He filled our backyard with a tension that Daddy finally decided was unnecessary.

One afternoon, as he was working in the yard, Daddy hailed a fellow walking down the street, and the two of them began a conversation. The young man he was talking to was known to all of us, as he daily walked by on his way somewhere. He wore a khaki-colored baseball cap with a longer-than-usual bill on it. He was usually whistling, appeared happy and never failed to give us a wave. As I watched this meeting play out in front of me—I was playing with my toy cars in the driveway—I saw Daddy reach in his pocket and pull out two or three dollars and hand it to the young man. They then disappeared behind the house. A couple of minutes later, the young man came running around the house holding Chuck's chain, with Chuck nipping at his heels. He headed north on Grove Street at full gallop, constantly looking over his shoulder to check on Chuck's progress at catching him. Daddy and I watched this drama until the man and Chuck disappeared over the hill. When they vanished, Daddy just went back to his yardwork, and I returned to playing "cars." I often wondered how that footrace came out, but I suspect it had a bad ending. No matter how it ended, Daddy got his money's worth, because we never saw Chuck again. I should also note: we never saw that young man again either. I hope he found a better way to get to where he was going, and didn't change his route due to a Chuck-induced injury that left him traumatized. That's enough about Chuck. This is Belle's story.

There were quite a few other dogs in the neighborhood, too, but only a couple of them were interesting enough to write about. My best bud growing up was Terry. His family had a mixed breed named Dot. Clearly, Dot was mostly collie, but she was sort of square in shape, not long and thin like most collies. She had long, thick, white hair with a large brown spot around her right eye. To Terry and his brother, Gaines, that spot looked like a dot, hence the name "Dot." I would have named her Spot, but so what? Terry and Dot lived across the street from us. The back of their house faced the front of ours. Dot hung out in their backyard and Belle hung out in our front yard. A hedgerow ran across the back of Terry's yard, providing visual privacy between the two yards. That visual barrier was a good thing, because Belle and Dot just plain couldn't

Terry with Belle's mortal enemy, Dot.

stand the sight of each other. Any time one of the dogs ventured across the dividing street, the dog whose territory had been encroached upon went ballistic and all hell broke loose. It was always a helluva fight but, inevitably, Dot won. Belle had short hair and Dot's bites drew blood. Anytime Belle bit, she just got a mouth full of white hair and air. In a dog fight, long, thick hair trumps courage. Without a doubt, Belle developed a Dot complex. Anytime you wanted to send Belle into a frantic rage, all you had to do was say the name "Dot." Belle would instantly charge to the edge of our property closest to Dot's domain and proceed to go nuts. She wasn't nutty enough to enter into Terry's yard, but she was, nonetheless, super hacked off. She would stay right in that spot slinging insults in Dot's direction until Robert or I called her off.

I never knew what caused the rift between Belle and Dot, but I suspect it was Stubby. Stubby was—like every other dog in our neighborhood—a mixed breed. Purebreds and lap dogs just didn't fit in South Marshall. His dominant parent had been a bulldog and, at first glance, everyone thought Stubby was a bulldog. He was pretty short, had broad shoulders and walked with a confident swagger. He knew he was hot stuff and he thought this was HIS neighborhood. On more than one occasion, Stubby went paw-to-paw with bigger dogs that had come sniffing around his turf and sent them home yelping in defeat. In his mind, this was "Stubbyville," and all the gals in this neighborhood were his private harem—Belle and Dot included. He was good-looking, charismatic, fearless and as tough as ten-year-old jerky, a combination that made him irresistible to lady dogs. Stubby wasn't monogamous, and most of the litters around South Marshall began as a twinkle in Stubby's eye. He must have had the best nose in Marshall because he was always the first Romeo to show up when a female came in heat. I think Belle and Dot were fighting over Stubby.

The geometry of Belle and Stubby making puppies together just didn't work. Belle was tall and Stubby was close to the ground. Belle had to make herself available to Stubby for

Belle trying to get Scotty to play with her.

them to get it on. She must have really loved Stubby because they had a bunch of litters together. The only other possibility was that Stubby was always the first to "get to" Belle when she came into season, meaning my beloved Belle might have been "easy" and would put out to any dog on four legs when the "heat" was on. I prefer to think of it as true love. Belle just couldn't have been morally challenged.

Once, when Daddy realized Belle was coming into season, he quickly loaded her in the car and drove her twenty or so miles to Aunt Bon's and Uncle Curly's house down on Caddo Lake. The plan was to chain her up in Curly's old hen house, which was no longer in use, to eliminate visits from horny male dogs. We would reclaim her when her season was over. Daddy drove home from there feeling good about his birth-control initiative. His good feelings lasted until about two AM, when we were awakened by the loud clanging of our water pipes under our house. We all jumped up thinking we were under siege. Daddy grabbed our flashlight and we all edged to our back door and eased outside to where the entrance to the crawlspace under our house was located. He quietly bent down and shined the light into the dark recesses of the unknown. What he saw was not a monster; it was Belle, who had been bumping her head on the pipes. I never have figured out if she kept bumping her head because she couldn't see in the dark, or if she just wanted to let us know she was back home. When she came outside, she was dragging the fifteen-foot-long chain Daddy and Curly had tied her up with. She had dragged it twenty miles across unknown territories in the black of night back home with nothing to guide her but her instincts. We were all flabbergasted by her courage and the strength of her attachment to us and her home. Daddy vowed he would never again separate her from the family. By the way, she did get pregnant again.

Stubby belonged to Bush Morgan, but he spent most of his time hanging around Ebb and Charlie Starke's house. Ebb and Charlie ran around with Stubby at their heels, and anytime you saw the Starke boys and Stubby wasn't with them, you knew he had caught the "scent" and was off courting.

By the time we had started high school, Belle, Dot and Stubby had passed on. Dot just got old, lay down and gave up the ghost. Age also took its toll on Stubby. He got to where he would come home from his sexual adventures cut up, bleeding and stumbling. It was sad to see Stubby in a swaggerless state. He just couldn't stave off the younger, stronger canine Don Juans like he once had. Stubby virtually crawled home from his last attempt at studliness and curled up underneath the large oak tree in the Stark's yard. His breathing was labored and his tongue just dangled out the side of his mouth. We all sat with Stubby but he didn't even acknowledge our presence. He just stared off into the distance. I'm sure he was reliving a life well-lived. He then closed his eyes and gave up his kingdom.

One time, Robert told me Belle's full name was Jezebel Cecilia De Carlo Eubanks. Cecilia was our Mother's middle name and De Carlo was the last name of the actress Yvonne De Carlo who my brother thought was the prettiest woman ever born. Also, Mother, Yvonne and Belle all had black hair. He just liked the name Jezebel. Belle, like our mother and the actress, was drop-dead gorgeous. I suppose that between the ages of five and fourteen, next to Mother and my Aunt Bon, I hugged Belle more than any other female. We were close and shared lots of hot, lazy summer afternoons just hanging around together.

When the end of the line came for Belle, she was in the midst of having puppies. The puppies didn't make it through the process and neither did Belle. She died in the arms of Robert, with me sitting beside him as he cradled her head. It hurt to let her go, even though it seemed to be a fitting way for Belle to bow out, as she had given birth to seventy-two puppies in her twelve years—most of them calling Stubby "Papa." She was as much a part of my upbringing as were my friends, my bicycle and my neighbors. Even today, I miss Belle. She's buried in the side yard of our old house on South Grove Street in Marshall.

Chapter 18
Bon, Curly, and Caddo Lake

Outside of my immediate family, no one had more influence on my formative years than my Aunt Bon and Uncle Curly. Outside of my hometown of Marshall, Texas, no *place* had more influence on my formative years than Caddo Lake. The fact that Bon and Curly lived at Caddo Lake brought these two powerful influences together and made their stories impossible to separate from each other. If I write this chapter well, you will flip its last page feeling the love, joy and adventure I experienced at Caddo Lake, while in the care of Bon and Curly.

Bon, whose full name was Bonnie Jewel Eubanks Kash, a.k.a., "The Jewel of the Eubanks Family," was one of my dad's older sisters. She was the most creative of the nine siblings and was quite a gifted writer, storyteller and maker-up of things for little kids to do when they were bored. She and Curly (real name Ernest) were childless, and so, it seemed to me, I was showered with their love and attention. Bon was one of the most intellectually curious people I ever met, and she packed a whole lot of knowledge into a brain that had to quit school after the eighth grade to work in the fields and take care of younger siblings. While Curly probably didn't even get to the eighth grade, his white-hair-rimmed bald head was filled with volumes of common sense and practical know-how. By the way, when he was younger, he had a full head of curly hair, hence the nickname Curly.

Bon and Curly lived at Caddo Lake in a house owned by the City of Marshall. They got to live there because Marshall got its water from Caddo Lake, and Curly ran the city's pump station that sucked water from the lake and sent it on its fifteen-mile trip to Marshall. The process started when Curly turned on pumps one, two or three. The pump station was located down the hill from their small, white-framed house, half way between the house and the Lake. It was a cavernous, concrete building that was in a constant state of hum from the whine of the working pumps. Curly checked the pumps regularly throughout each twenty-four-hour cycle, and, at night, you could hear Curly's voice bouncing off the concrete pump house walls as he sang the blues. He had a really good voice, and I remember lying in bed listening to him belt out my favorites like "Muleskinner Blues" and "Old Man River." I loved going to the station with him, because he often let me turn on a pump or turn one off. He always made me feel important when I did so.

Caddo Lake was not a small lake. It was—and is—a 26,000-acre lake that straddles the Texas-Louisiana line. The forty-square-mile lake is 50 percent in Texas and 50 percent in Caddo Parish, Louisiana. The Texas half is about sixteen miles outside of Marshall. Growing up, I just naturally assumed it was a Texas lake, but that kind of fits the way us Texans view the world around us. Caddo was named for the Caddo Indians (Caddoans), who lived and farmed at or around the Lake for hundreds and hundreds of years. As a child playing in the dirt near the Lake, I found three different arrowheads left behind by the Indians. I still have them. Caddo is the only natural lake in Texas and the largest natural lake in the South. Caddo Lake is not a big open-water lake—anything but. It's an infinite number of bayous, sloughs, swamps and ponds, connected by barely navigable "ditches" and small canals. It's home to one of the largest Cypress forests in the world, and all of the Cypress trees, both in the Lake and around it, are liberally draped by Spanish Moss. The bayous, the sloughs, the swamps, the trees and the moss give Caddo an eeriness and a mystical quality unmatched by other lakes. While everybody who sees Caddo speaks of its beauty and seductive power, they admit to being somewhat intimidated by its many hidden dangers. While it's full of bass, trophy-sized gar and catfish, goggle eye, pike and bream, it is also full of alligators, coral snakes, rattlers, copperheads and water moccasins. Fishermen on Caddo are well-advised to carry an empty coffee can to use when they have to pee. Pulling up on land to get out and accommodate one's bladder is ill-advised. The poisonous snakes, gators and wild angry hogs are too apt to turn one's "pause that refreshes" into a harrowing experience. If creepy, crawly and grunting things don't make the hair on the back of your neck stand up, well, how about this fact? For many, many years, hundreds of Bigfoot sightings at Caddo Lake have made the news. Uncle Curly once told me Caddo Lake was like a beautiful, selfish woman: wonderful to look at, but dangerous as hell. Caddo owns a spot in the history of the oil industry, in that the first over-water oil well in the world was drilled in Caddo Lake. Old derricks dot the Lake's surface, but most have been converted to duck blinds now. I always had good luck catching white perch (crappie) around the old footings.

I enjoyed spending time with Bon and Curly at the lake for as long as I can remember. My first memories include Bon scrubbing me in the bath tub so hard I thought my skin would come off. When I complained, she told me to "hush," or she would use Curly's Lava soap on me. For those of you unfamiliar with Lava Soap, it is pumice-filled and will take chrome off of a bumper. I recall crawling in bed with her and having her tell me stories she had made up just for me. She had several stories, each with its own cast of characters. One was the adventures of the frog, "Lickety Split" and his buddy, "Strombolie," a dim-witted turtle. Then there were the tales of "Wishy-Washy," an ambitious rooster that spent a lot of time trying to catch "Squoosh Bug" and his little friends, "Doodle

Bug," "Lady Bug" and "Slimy" the worm. I don't remember the stories, but I vividly recall the characters and the excitement their adventures brought me as I drifted off to sleep.

Walt Disney saw Caddo as a rare beauty and filmed several movie and serial scenes there. He even filmed one full-length movie on Caddo. I believe it was called *Swamp Boy*, but don't hold me to it.

I loved Bon and Curly equally, so it was hard for me to pick which one to sleep with when I was small. I never wanted to hurt either of their feelings by selecting one over the other. Truth be known, they each probably pulled for me to pick the other so they could get a good night's sleep. I chose to sleep with Bon most often, because Curly was a lousy story teller and often drifted off to sleep before I did. Also, on cold nights, Bon would heat bricks in the fireplace, wrap them in towels and place them at the foot of the bed under the covers to keep our feet warm.

I vividly recall one night when Curly and I snuck outside while Bon was sleeping. We quietly turned on the outside water hose, eased around to the open window closest to Bon's bed, and sprayed her through the screen. While we were yucking it up, Bon locked us out and made us sit outside for what seemed like hours before she took pity on us and let us in. Another time when I was sleeping with Curly, Bon snuck outside, crept up to our window and scratched on the screen while screeching like a panther. That time, she scared both of us so bad even Curly screamed. They kept me entertained.

Bon was a nature lover and often took me on long walks. We usually stayed on the one-lane blacktop road that ran the mile or so between the house and the Farm-to-Market road that connected Jefferson to Karnack. Our main mission was to identify birds and their calls. There were many, many varieties of birds at Caddo and Bon seem to know them all. She always seemed most thrilled when we saw a bluebird. She said they brought good luck and God's love. Quite often, we would take empty lard cans with us and gather wild blackberries with which she would make a great cobbler. Our walks taught me many things, such as the importance of giving skunks and porcupines a wide berth, and walking in the middle of the road so as to not surprise a snake that might be lying just off the road's surface. Also, she taught me to never stick my hand into or under places I couldn't see into because there was no telling what kind of creature may be hiding in there. East Texas had lots of inhospitable varmints such as scorpions, snakes and spiders. She also taught me to identify poison oak, poison ivy and bull nettle—all three of which could bring you lots of woes. As an aside, brother Robert told me that if I ever suffered from the effects of bull nettle, to get someone to pee on it and the misery would subside. I never knew whether to believe brother Robert.

For many years, Bon and Curly had chickens and guineas. The chickens were Brown Leghorns and Road Island Reds. The guineas were just guineas. They were interesting to look at and listen to, but they were so skittish, you couldn't get close to 'em. Curly built a really neat henhouse adjoining one side of his garage, and every day Bon gathered eggs from the hens, which sometimes acted as though they didn't want her to have them. I always stood behind her at egg-gathering time because I didn't trust the hens. The henhouse stunk to high heaven and its floor was always covered in chicken poop. From my childish perspective, it looked—and smelled—like all hens did were to lay eggs and crap. I never volunteered to help Curly clean out the coop.

The chicken flock also had two or three roosters at all times, and, to put it mildly, they were meaner than rabid coons. They had one rooster for a spell that whenever he heard the kitchen screen door open, he came tearing around the corner to attack my little butt with fiery conviction. If it was Bon or Curly coming outside, he went on about his business. If it was me slipping through the door, the race and the fight were on. I don't know if I looked like a competing rooster to him or what, but his hostility was clearly focused on me. He always went straight to pecking at my ankles, often soaking my white socks with ankle blood. I tried to outrun him but couldn't. I kicked him, but he came right back. This battle went on for several visits to the lake, and I never won once. Then I returned to Bon and Curly's one time and the rooster warrior was gone. I don't know if they ate him, shot him or if he picked on a hawk and lost the fight. I didn't care why he was gone, I was just glad to reclaim my territory.

As I got a little older, Bon once gave me the egg basket and told me to go get the eggs out of the hen house. She stoked my confidence and told me to just stick my hand under the hen and take the eggs from each nest. I nervously completed the task and was so proud and excited I ran from the henhouse toward the house to show Bon all the eggs I had found. As I rounded the corner, my feet slipped on the pine straw, and the eggs flew in one direction and I tumbled in the other. Every single one of them broke, and I was petrified by my failure. In haste, I covered the broken eggs with pine straw and slowly headed to the kitchen door. When I went in, Bon asked me where the eggs were. I told her the hens hadn't laid any. She could tell I was fibbing because she knew her hens and because my face was as red as a beet. It didn't help that I wouldn't look her in the eye either. She said nothing except that we would try again in the morning. Several days later, while we were sitting on the front porch having a glass of iced tea, she gently informed me that honor and the truth were far more valuable than a few eggs. I understood.

Each new year, Bon and Curly got new, large calendars from the feed store. The calendars had color pictures of the different breeds of chickens one year and pictures of different breeds of pigs the next. Those calendars became teaching tools for Bon, and, by the time I started the first grade, I was the only kid in school who could identify all of the kinds of chickens and pigs. Nobody cared, or was particularly impressed with my peculiar knowledge. Ruth Ann, Sally and the other girls seemed like they couldn't care less that I knew the differences among a Hampshire, a Poland China and a Duroc pig. Curly had taught me the colors of horses such as roan, chestnut, palomino, bay, dapple and paint, but that didn't impress the girls either. Rats. I still enjoyed my rides through the countryside with Curly, during which we talked about the livestock and animals we saw and our trips to the livestock auctions together. He loved to look at mules, and now I love to look at mules. Before he moved to the lake, Curly and Bon had a small house outside of Marshall and a couple of acres he farmed. He had a mule named Dinah that constantly jumped its fence and had to be retrieved from their neighbor's, the Hallock's, garden. Curly eventually sold Dinah.

Uncle Curly had been married before he hooked up with Aunt Bon. His first marriage produced two daughters, one of whom lived in Marshall. The Marshall daughter was Irene, and she and her husband Robert had a daughter named Ila Pat that was just a year younger than me. The fact that we weren't blood relatives didn't cross my mind. I always thought of them as family, and of Ila Pat as my cousin. Sometimes Bon and Curly hosted Ila Pat and me at the same time. We played together a lot—well, at least as much as a boy and girl could tolerate. One time we both loaded our bikes in the back of Curly's 1939 Chevy pick-up and headed for the lake. We hadn't been there long when we decided to ride down to the lake's edge for a look around. Ila Pat was much less adventurous than me, so she had to muster a whole bunch of courage to embark on such a venture. The two-rutted dirt road that led from the pump house to the channel was barely passible, and as we pedaled along it, the waist-high weeds and briars slapped and grabbed at our legs; but we made it. This "icky" weed and briar action ate away at Ila Pat's comfort with this whole adventure. We then followed a more navigable dirt road to Long's Fishing Camp. On the way, we encountered quite a few chug holes, each of which was full of water from the previous night's rain. While we were able to steer around most of them, there was one big one that ran completely across the road. As I assessed the hazard, its depth concerned me. My solution was to send Ila Pat and her blue and white bike on ahead of me. I told her the mud puddle was just that, a shallow puddle. In faith, she plowed into it, and she and her bike damn near disappeared into the muddy pool. She then tipped over. With my help, she eventually crawled and bawled her way out of the "puddle" and focused her full attention on the hissy-fit she was throwing. I helped her wipe the mud from her face, and when she finally quit spitting muddy water and regained her faculties, we started the long walk home, pushing our bikes up the steep hill. Neither one of us said a word the entire long walk back to the house on top of the hill. I don't remember getting in trouble over this incident, but I do remember having to wash Ila Pat's bike, while she was getting one of Bon's scrub jobs in the bathtub. I don't think Ila Pat ever brought her bike back to the lake.

Ila Pat and I usually slept with Bon. She slept between Bon and me because she was afraid of the night sounds we always heard through the open windows of Bon's bedroom. Sounds like the call of the whip-poor-will, the bob white and the owls kept her spooked. The muffled sounds of nosy visitors like possums, raccoons and armadillos, when blended with the purr made by the wind rushing through the pines, seemed to keep Ila Pat in a state of fidgety nervousness until she fell asleep. We went on bunking together until Bon informed us we were too old to sleep with our legs intertwined. Bon moved to the middle of the bed. Ila Pat seemed to outgrow overnight visits to the lake. I never did.

That same two-rut road or path that led from the pump station to the lake was the only way to the water. We often lugged our fishing poles and can full of fresh-dug worms to the lake's edge and fished for bream and goggle-eye. It was where the intake for the pump station was located because it was the deepest spot on Caddo Lake. The Little Cypress River fed into Caddo and our water frontage was right on the river's main channel. Curly told me the water at the intake was over forty feet deep. Needless to say, the words "be careful" were the last words I always heard when I went fishing.

One summer afternoon, Curly, brother Robert and I were walking the path to the lake when a large water moccasin—sometimes called a cottonmouth—crawled into our path and glared at us. It was close enough to scare the pudding out of us, but Robert quickly drew his 22-caliber pistol from its holster and hip-shot the snake right between the eyes. The moccasin quivered a little bit then died. The speed with which Robert drew, shot and hit the snake amazed Uncle Curly. He told everyone about the incident, and Robert achieved hall-of-fame status among all of our family and friends. It was no fluke. Robert—then eighteen years old—was a fast draw with a deadeye aim. He was the undisputed best shot with any firearm in our big family. He also had the best arm and aim in the family when throwing baseballs, ice picks, knives and rocks. At one of our many family reunions at Bon and Curly's, all of the men were sitting in lawn chairs in front of the house while the women were busy readying something to eat when an armadillo scurried by about forty or fifty feet in front of us. Robert quickly grabbed a rock and fired a Bob Feller-like fast ball at the varmint. The rock not only hit the armadillo, it penetrated the critter's armor and killed it instantly; a difficult feat, to say the least. Now before you animal rights folks jump my bones about animal cruelty, remember this was in the 1950s in rural Texas.

Family reunions at the lake often had thirty to fifty kinfolks and another ten to twenty friends who felt like family. The amount of food the women produced from Bon's tiny kitchen was mind-boggling. They varied the food, but the fare I most remember was fried fish, hush puppies, corn fritters, watermelon and homemade ice cream. Sometimes as many as five or six ice cream freezers were being hand-cranked under the pine trees at the same time. The little kids were assigned to sit on the freezers while the older kids cranked the handles. The closer the ice cream got to being ready, the harder the crank was to turn. When I finally got big enough to be promoted to cranker, I strutted around like a bandy rooster. However, after about ten minutes of cranking, I was worn out and ready to go play. Curly always set up horseshoe-throwing stakes, and he buried Vienna sausage cans with their open tops at ground level for throwing washers for our get-togethers. I much preferred competing at one of the games to cranking the ice cream freezers, but Daddy wasn't big on work-release programs.

(L to R) Cousin Becky, Cousin Pat, Scotty, Cousin Sue, and a seldom-seen distant cousin whose name slips my mind, sitting in a porch swing at a family gathering at Bon's and Curly's house on Caddo Lake. The 1956 Pontiac in the background is the one Daddy let me take to school in the sixth grade.

While the food was delightful, the highlight of the reunions was the family fellowship and hearing the men tell the stories of their past. Daddy's sisters Vina, Bon and Phyllis had great senses of humor and were tremendous story tellers in their own rights, but, for the most part, they were used to verify the stories told by the men.

Grandpa Eubanks, who lived in Muskogee, Oklahoma, came to some of the reunions. He had been a sharecropper most of his life, and his face had been fried and wrinkled by too many days in the sun. He wore a straight-brimmed little Stetson and looked like a wizened old Indian chief. He sat among the men just grinning and smoking his hand-rolled cigarettes or drawing on his corncob pipe. He said very little, but he always had a twinkle in his eye that hinted that he might be up to mischief. There were always a couple of stray cats and country dogs hanging around Bon and Curly's, and they hung close to folks hoping for a food handout. One time, Grandpa told me to grab a cat and he would show me how to have a little fun with it. Being the obedient grandson, I did as instructed and, at his request, I handed the squirming cat over to him. He then ran a pipe cleaner through his pipe and rubbed the nicotine-laced pipe cleaner under the cat's tail. The squirming cat turned into the flying cat, and when he finally hit the ground, he tore off in no particular direction screaming at the top of his lungs. He finally set an eastward course, and I'll bet that cat didn't stop running until he hit the Louisiana line. I was dumbfounded by the spectacle I had just seen, but Grandpa laughed until his eyes watered. Grandpa held some kind of power over me because on another visit to the ;ake, he talked me into shooting my own lake dog, Spot, in the butt with my bb gun. The butt shot didn't hurt Spot, but still . . . Spot was destined to get shot, because when Curly caught him killing chickens, he promptly shot him between the eyes with his antique .22. I was standing behind Curly during the execution, but it didn't bother me all that much. I understood the rationale. When you had chickens, stray dogs and cats lurking around usually spelled trouble.

Curly had been trying to catch one old stray cat for several days but could never corner him or get a clear shot at him. Then one morning, I saw the cat crawl under the small back porch off the kitchen. When I told Curly where the cat was hiding, he grabbed a cherry bomb from the sack load of them he used for blowing-up stumps. Next, he quietly went through the kitchen and crept onto the porch. He then stood in the middle of the porch so he could see the cat whichever side he came out from. Lastly, he lit the cherry bomb and held it, waiting for the cat to exit from under the porch. I guess Curly forgot that when the fuse burns out, the cherry bomb is going to explode whether the cat has moved or not. The cat stayed still, the fuse burned out, and the cherry bomb blew up in Curly's right hand. Cherry bombs were powerful firecrackers, and the explosion sent Curly cussing and dancing all over the back yard. The cat then casually walked out from under the porch, stopped, watched Curly dispassionately for a second or two, then moseyed off. Bon took an old clean rag, drenched it in coal oil, and wrapped his hand. He lost use of that hand for several days, but he learned a lesson about holding on too long to things that could hurt you. This place is as good as any to tell you that Bon treated pretty near all sprains, cuts, bites and bruises with coal oil, Campho-Phenique or hydrogen peroxide. Those curatives pretty much made up the country medicine chest in the 1950s.

Curly was a very patient man. His patience was most always a good thing, even though being so patient in waiting for the cat to exit from under the porch while holding the lit cherry bomb proved that being overly patient can be a painful experience. An example of Curly's patience paying off for me occurred when he decided to hand carve me a baseball bat. Before I describe the process he employed in carving my bat, I should tell you that at that point in my life—age ten or so—baseball was my burning passion. When at home in Marshall, my highest summer priority was to play baseball. I had made the Little League Giants at age nine, a rarity for a nine-year-old because you were competing with boys who were mostly ten, eleven or twelve. In those days, you were not just put on a team. One had to go through competitive tryouts, and that process always sent a lot of kids home with a sense of failure and a case of the blues. At any rate, I was a Giant, and I was either practicing with my team, playing a game with my team or riding around Marshall looking for a pick-up game.

When I was at the lake, there were no baseball games, so I started passing the time and practicing my hitting by batting rocks. For bats, I used Curly's old axe handles, Bon's old broomsticks (which Curly sawed off for me), or limbs that I trimmed down. I would stand in a pile of rocks and swat them off toward the swamp for hours at a time. I judged each hit as to whether it was a single, a double, a triple or a home run, based on how hard and how far I knocked the rock. Pop-ups, dribblers and swings-and-misses were outs. My competing imaginary teams were all-stars from the major league teams. If the star was left-handed, I batted left-handed. If he was right-handed, I hit right-handed. If he was a switch-hitter, like Mickey Mantle, I hit both ways. I can still recall that Early Wynn was my winningest pitcher, and Eddie Mathews won the most home-run crowns. To understand the intensity with which I "batted" rocks, well, I guess you would have had to have been there. Curly was there, and he knew this rock-hitting passion was my version of the major leagues. He also knew that after my make-do bats had come in contact with thousands of rocks, they were chewed in two and no longer useable. That fact inspired my loving uncle to carve me a bat that would last longer than an axe handle. Since he wanted to surprise me when the bat was finished, he never told me what he was doing and he only worked on it in my absence. Before I go on about the bat, let me add that when I wasn't at the lake, Curly would push his wheelbarrow around several acres of land filling it with good "battin' rocks." I would arrive at the lake later to find a huge pile of fresh "baseballs" for Ted Williams to slug over the imaginary right-field wall.

Now, back to the bat. Curly decided that to give the bat durability he would use oak wood. He started with a carefully selected oak fence post and went to work on it. He used a hand lathe to give it a rough bat shape. Next, he used his pocket knife to refine the shape. Lastly, he used shards of glass to smooth the wood into a perfect, smooth baseball bat. Bon later told me Curly had worked on the bat one entire winter and spring. As I said earlier, Curly was a very patient man. When he finished it, it was a perfect thirty-two-inch-long bat. When he presented it to me, I was astounded by both its quality and by the incredible love Curly showed to me by making this bat for me. I never told Curly, but oak is a very heavy wood and the bat was too heavy for me to swing as a ten-year-old. However, I never let on to Curly that the bat was giving me a double hernia. I didn't, in any way, want to hurt his feelings, so I used the bat all the time. By using it constantly, I got stronger and stronger, and I got to where I could wield it with grace and efficiency. Eventually, my constant rock-bashing even wore through the heavy oak. I kept the stub as a reminder of Curly's love for me until I got married. I wish I still had it.

I probably haven't done a great job of transitioning from one thought to the next in this chapter. That's because my thoughts about Bon and Curly and Caddo Lake come at me in such a fast and furious pace they are hard to nail down in any particular order. There are many more things I'd like to record, but I fear I'm wearing you out on the subject. I haven't even mentioned the time my friend Scooter Adams spent the weekend with me at the lake and we walked six miles on the railroad track to Karnack, sat down on the front porch of T. J. Taylor's grocery store and ate the lunch Bon had made for us. T. J. Taylor was Lady Bird Johnson's daddy. After lunch, we walked the six miles back to the house. Our mission on that trek was to find fossils among the many rocks that made up the railbed. We did find lots of fossils—of which I still have a couple—but our big adventure was stoning to death a big copperhead snake that was sunning on the rocks. We also ventured off the railroad long enough to find a pocket full of good-luck buckeyes.

I also nearly forgot to tell you about the time I went along with Curly to watch him chop firewood in the lake bottom. When we got to where Curly had been working for several days, I plopped down on a stump and watched him swing his axe. During a quick catch-your-breath pause, Curly looked over at me and turned white as a sheet. I recognized fear in his eyes, but I sat there looking at him. He slowly edged over to me and calmly held his hand out to me. When I placed my hand in his, he yanked me off that stump and attacked it viciously with his axe. When I looked at the stump, I realized why. I had been sharing my stump seat with a very venom-ous coral snake—a coral snake that was now chopped into about ten pieces.

I remember going to tent gospel singings with Bon and Curly, and I remember the countless evening hours we spent in front of their little fireplace with their Philco radio dial set on the Grand Ole Opry or the Louisiana Hayride. I remember singing along with Slim Whitman, Little Jimmy Dickens, Hank Williams, Hank Snow and Sonny James. I remember switching over to a gospel music station and listening to my favorites, the Stamps Quartet. I remember the tears in Aunt Bon's eyes when she heard "Amazing Grace" or "The Old Rugged Cross."

Once, when I was fourteen, my four-year-old nephew, Homer III, and I were spending the weekend at Bon and Curly's, and everything was going fine until Bon had to correct "The Third" on something he had done. He didn't take well to that particular scolding and swelled up like a toad and put on his best pout face. He announced to all he was running away. Bon told him she would make him a sandwich to take with him, as he would probably get hungry while he was "on the road." After making it, she tied it up in a bandana and tied the bandana on a long stick so he could carry it resting the stick on his shoulder hobo style. He then started off walking down the little road that led from the house, glancing back over his shoulder at regular intervals in hopes someone was coming to fetch him. Bon, Curly and I just waved at him and yelled for him to be careful. After a few more steps, Homer turned around to us and, between sobs, informed us he might get run over by "a big ole' truck." No one moved, so he turned around and continued his slow walk toward who-knows-where. At this point, we all looked at each other, nodded and retrieved our boy before the "big ole' truck" could harm him. All was fine then.

I will remember many events and happenings that happened at Bon and Curly's on Caddo Lake long after I've quit writing these memoirs, but it's time to shut this chapter down. Bon and Curly retired and left the Lake in the early 1960s, bringing my closeness to Caddo lake to a close. It had been my Disneyland throughout my most formative years. Adventure after adventure stocked my experience bank—a bank from which I still make regular withdrawals.

Bon and Curly both died in the late 1960s, leaving a hole in my heart I wouldn't dare let anyone else fill. I still have a few mementos from the times I spent with them. I have notes Bon wrote to me filled with her memories of my childhood, each recalling incidents she found amusing, such as the time she taught me to skip rocks on a pond when I was four. Another recalls her telling me that when raindrops hit water, the resultant splash was simply raindrops dancing. I also have a very small, little, green enamel teapot that she always served my half-a-Coke from during our "tea" breaks on hot afternoons. Tea Time was a valued ritual we shared. I have cutouts in the shape of my body she made by having me lie down on brown, dry, goods wrapping paper and outlining my body with crayons. Each cutout bears my name and my age at the time of the outlining. Even now, I can unfurl the cutouts and see how tall I was at a given time in my childhood.

Aunt Bon, Uncle Curly and Caddo Lake: I was so blessed to have them in my life.

Chapter 19
Bidgie, Midgie, Dooley, and Dud

There were four girls who lived within a stone's throw from our house on South Grove Street who were named Bidgie York, Midgie Miller, Dud Hynson and Dooley Hynson. These were smart, pretty, likeable girls who, for some reason, went through life in Marshall with those weird—albeit sort of cute—names. Bidgie even won the Miss Marshall Pageant, so she was not only pretty, she was also talented and shapely. I guess all of the names were nicknames, but I never heard any of them called by any name other than the ones I just noted. I'm in no way making fun of those girls; I'm just using their monikers to introduce this chapter on some of the nicknames that were prominent in Marshall in the 1950s and '60s. I know every town in America had folks with unusual names or nicknames, but meeting some of Marshall's may help you understand my hometown a little better.

Remembering that Marshall, Texas was, in all truth, a Southern town, it won't come as a surprise that in the '40s, '50s and '60s, there were boatloads of folks with double names. We had more than our share of double-namers, including the following: Mellie Jo, Ila Pat, Donna Jean, Jerri Lynn, Mary Katherine, Roy Lee, Eddie Joe (a.k.a. "Mouse"), Carol Ann, Ruth Ann, John Mark, Tommy Lee, Mary Jane, Mary Lou, Jimmy Ray, Betty Jane, Teddie Lee, Mary Grace, Sara Lynn, Jo Lynn, Lola Faye, Jimmie Faye, Betty Lou, Davey Lee and Peggy Sue. All of the above-mentioned were actual classmates of mine, and I just pulled them right out of an old part of my brain. No telling how many more I could come up with if I took a few thoughtful minutes, but you get the point. In small town Southern America—and Texas, too—double names were in fashion.

Like every other place, we also had our share of Bubbas, Butchs, Woodys, Buddys and Sonnys. The "Butch" I remember best was Butch Kennedy. He was a great high school football and baseball player and as tough as an old boot. He was a friend of mine, and his real name was Joe Billy, so he would have made my nickname chapter regardless of which name we settled on for him. Butch was a year older than me, so he got his driver's license a year before I did. He and I double dated a few times, and the first time he picked me up, I noticed he had a bottle of Old Spice cologne in the seat next to him. After we had driven about two minutes on the way to pick up our dates, I understood why the Old Spice was sitting between us. His old, green, 1952 Plymouth's right front floorboard had rusted out and the toxic exhaust fumes from his busted muffler rose through the holey floorboard and stunk up the inside of the car something fierce. When the stench became unbearable, Butch would liberally sprinkle the Old Spice onto the muffler through the hole in the floorboard, thinking it would help the ambience inside the Plymouth. It didn't. He kept all the windows rolled down, so I guess that's what kept us from dying from carbon monoxide poisoning. I decided then and there that double dating with Butch in the winter was out of the question. Freezing to death or dying from carbon monoxide poisoning was a choice I didn't want to make.

Right around the corner from our house lived a boy named Bush Morgan. Bush was about seven or eight years older than me. He was a nice boy, played quarterback and was real popular. One time I asked my brother Robert if "Bush" was his real name or just a nickname. He told me it was a "temporary" name, and that when Bush became an adult, his name would become "Tree." I walked away from our conversation a bit thoughtful, but satisfied with the answer. It was a year or two later that I realized Robert was jiving me and that "Bush" was his real name. I went through a similar situation when Robert started running around with a guy named Foots Wagner. I wanted to ask Robert if his new friend's "real" name was Foots, but I figured he would tell me that it also was just a temporary name, and that when he became an adult, his name would become "Yards." I was too smart to be fooled twice by my smart-ass brother. My other brother, Homer, had a life-long friend named Choppie Wendt. He wasn't just Choppie, he was Choppie, Jr., so there were two of them. When I asked Homer if "Choppie" was a nickname, he told me that, in fact, it was. He added that it was the nickname for "Chop." I had two smart-ass brothers.

Daddy had several friends in Marshall who had unusual names. When we had our grocery store, one of our butcher's name was "Sut" Allen. I guess "Sut" was short for Sutton, but I can't swear to it. Sut resigned his butcher's job at Eubanks Quality Foods to eventually become Marshall's Chief of Police and was replaced by a nice man named Allen Power, who went by "Doc." There's nothing too unusual about the name Doc Power, but his cousin was named Will. Get it, Will Power? Most folks called him "Willpower." "Willpower" had a brother who worked in the men's department at Weisman's. He was known as "Hip" Power. I don't know where Mr. Power got the name "Hip," but I looked him over and both his hips looked normal to me.

One of our regular customers at the grocery store was a man named Pie Davis. If Mr. Davis had another first name besides "Pie," no one knew it. Pie's daughter, Diane, and I went to elementary school together. I wish I had asked her if her dad's "real" name was Pie, but I never got around to it. Two other well-known Marshallites from my dad's generation were "Bunny" Young and "Beer" Smith. I put their names in quotation marks, but "Bunny" and "Beer" may have been their real first names. One of Daddy's closest friends was Tibby Barnes. I can't think of a formal name from which "Tibby" would have sprung unless his given name was Tibson or Tibbington or something like that. And then there was "Cap" Solomon. "Cap" owned an auto salvage yard on Highway 80, and if you needed to replace a lost hubcap, Solomon's was your best bet. Maybe "Cap" was short for hubcap, or maybe he always wore a cap. I'll never know why he was called "Cap."

Among Daddy's cadre of drinking buddies was the set of twins named Buck and Bish Little I mentioned before. They were somewhat notorious in and around Marshall because, reputedly, they would cut you up or shoot you in a heartbeat. They weren't big men, but both had whiskey-worn, scarred faces that let everyone around them know they weren't strangers to trouble. Buck was a deputy sheriff and wore a gun. Bish was a pipeliner who kept a straight-edged razor in his boot. Everyone knew the gun and the razor had been used on numerous occasions, so the lore around Buck and Bish was duly earned. I remember Bish as a very nice man. He and Daddy were good buds, so that made him my friend, too. Daddy had first cousins from the hills of Arkansas whose names were Wub and Fed, so we didn't have to look far to find kin folks with "rare" names.

Marshall had some other noteworthy characters with odd names. First to mind was Piggy Byrne. He became one of the wealthiest guys in town through insurance, oil and gas. He was prominent in Marshall socially and politically, yet he was "Piggy." I'm sure he had a "real" name, but I don't think even his closest friends knew what it was. It must have been a doozy for him to choose Piggy over it. I always wondered if he got the name "Piggy" because he was selfish, because of his table manners, because he oinked when he thought no one was around or because he looked like a pig. I guess I'll never know.

There was another character in Marshall that deserves an introduction. His name was Pinkie. Pinkie was an albino black man whose skin was baby-pig pink and his eyes were ice blue. His hair had the texture of most black men's hair but it was snow white, even when Pinkie was young. His memorable appearance, when coupled with the fact that he didn't have a car and walked all over town pushing his lawn mower, made him very well-known to everyone in town. He made his money mowing lawns, and he had built-up a pretty good list of clients. Problem was, when Pinkie had money in his pocket, he generally made a beeline for a bootlegger. Pinkie would find a nice shade tree, settle under it, and polish off a pint of Old Crow. When the bottle was finished, Pinkie usually was, too. However, he would get to his feet, prop himself against the handle of his lawnmower and head home. He lived somewhere out off of Carthage Highway, better known as U.S. 59, a major North-South highway in Texas, so he had a long walk home. Pinkie usually stayed in the right-of-way and out of harm's way. Sometimes folks would see Pinkie passed out beside the highway, too. However, on one occasion, Pinkie and his lawnmower kept swerving into the traffic lane, creating all sorts of traffic issues and horn-honking. Finally, a Marshall policeman pulled Pinkie over, and—are you ready for this?—gave Pinkie a citation for Walking While Intoxicated. I often wondered what some of the motorists thought when they encountered a pink, blue-eyed, black man erratically pushing a lawnmower down a major national highway. Thanks for the memories, Pinkie.

There was a short little man in Marshall who, like Pinkie, didn't drive, so he walked all around town. His name was Shorty Scott. I suppose if you stretched him out, he might have hit the five-foot mark. He was built like a Weeble Wobble and looked like the little dude pictured on the Monopoly Game cards. Despite his cartoonish physique, he was always dressed to the nines in slacks and a starched, long-sleeved, white shirt. His favorite thing to do was to attend all the Little League and Babe Ruth League baseball games, which were held at our City Park complex. He came early and stayed late. When the lights went off at the park after all the games, Shorty would walk off to the north heading home. I always watched him very closely. Why? Well, I watched him closely because my older brothers used to tell me Shorty Scott was my real daddy and that Mother and Daddy adopted me because Shorty didn't want me. That, they said, was why I was named Scott. I always figured they were kidding me, but I also figured I ought to watch Shorty just in case they weren't kidding.

In addition to all the double-named classmates I had, there were other classmates with names or nicknames worthy of mention. I'll run through a few of them for you. In elementary school, we had a girl whose name was Biddie Green. As old as I now am, I've never heard of another soul named Biddie. One of the better halfbacks on our junior high football team, the Mighty Mites, was "Hobo" Harbour. I think his real name was Gilbert, but I never heard him called anything but "Hobo." The quarterback of that same team was "Deacon" Lewis. "Deacon," legally Malcolm, played quarterback for our high school team, also, and then played one year for Texas University. There was a ragged old country boy who went by "Buckshot" George. He and his older brother, Pete, were both a bit on the small side, but they both seemed to always have a "mad" on. I always figured messing with one of them was akin to kicking a hornet's nest, so I gave them a wide berth. We also had two "Scooters," "Scooter" Adams (real name Ollie) and "Scooter"—David—Newton, whose older brother was "Fig" Newton. Ronnie Salmon was far better-known as "Fish," for obvious reasons. He was also known as "Sloth," because he moved so slowly. The smartest boy my age in Marshall was "Doc" Roberts, a.k.a. Gary, who went on to be voted "Most Intelligent" in our high school class. "Doc" was a small boy who wore glasses. Come to think of it, he sort of reminded one of Doc, of Seven Dwarfs fame. Despite being super intelligent, Doc had a great sense of humor and a quick wit. He was a fun nerd.

I can't really tell you why I felt the urge to write a chapter on names and nicknames. Maybe it had something to do with my Texas roots. Remember, we had a Texas Governor whose last name was Hogg. He reputedly named his two daughters Ima and Ura. How's that for a sense of humor? What makes the matter even more laughable is the fact that there was no daughter named "Ura." It seems that when Mr. Hogg was running for office, he was often accompanied on the campaign trail by his daughter Ima and her best friend. The two girls were very close and had a strong physical resemblance. When Mr. Hogg would introduce the girls at campaign events, he would introduce them as his twin daughters, Ima and Ura. The "twins" became part of Texas lore, even though Ura was pure fiction.

I don't know why nicknames and odd names seemed more prevalent in the South than they did in the North, but they did. What if John D. Rockefeller had been called "Scooter" Rockefeller? Or maybe it had been "Daffy" Taft instead of William Howard Taft? What if Abraham Lincoln went by "Hobo" Lincoln? You get the picture. Would we ever have elected a man named "Buckshot" Kennedy from Massachusetts?

Chapter 20

Mary Ellen Did Wear a Bra and Scooter Pooted

My mother had a cousin from Illinois named Lawrence. Lawrence had never married and seemed to relish his freedom. When he wasn't working on pipelines, he rode trains all over America. Since he never paid for a ticket, Lawrence was technically a hobo. If you were a hobo, Marshall was easy to get to because it was a big part of the Texas and Pacific Railroad and it had railroad tracks from all over America converging in it. Hobos were notorious for hitting a town and going door-to-door begging for food or money. They generally knocked on the back doors of the homes which were, more often than not, doors that led right to the kitchen. If the housewife who opened the door gave the hobo food or money, the hobo would mark that door with an "X" with chalk. This "X" told other hobos the folks living in this house would "help out."

Back to cousin Lawrence. We never knew when Lawrence was going to show up and spend a night or two with us. He was always welcomed at our house because he brought news about other relatives of ours who were scattered around the country. He was a quiet, tall, polite man who always wore a khaki shirt and khaki pants. They always looked neat and wrinkle-free, so he must not have rolled around much when he slept in a boxcar. I never knew much about cousin Lawrence, but I do know he liked mashed potatoes.

I learned of his fondness for mashed potatoes because of what happened one night as we all sat around our dining table to share dinner. Mother, Daddy, brothers Homer and Robert, cousin Lawrence and I kicked off dinner by waiting patiently for the food to be passed to us. That particular night, I was on the tail end of the food receiving line so I was watching the portions everyone took to make sure there was enough left over for me when each dish made it to the end of the line. I was always hungry, so I took this vigil very seriously. Everything was looking good until the mashed potatoes got to cousin Lawrence who was the last stop before me. It seemed to me that our hobo cousin was taking more than his share of mashed potatoes, so, in near panic mode, I blurted out, "Hey, save some of those mashed potatoes for me!" A deadly quiet consumed the room and all eyes were focused on me. After a seemingly eternal silence, the sound of Daddy's chair scooting away from the table signaled trouble ahead for yours truly. Daddy calmly—but firmly—gripped my upper arm and removed me from my chair.

Once he had me in the bedroom behind a closed door, Daddy wore my little nine-year-old butt out with his strong right hand. It wasn't over. He was then joined by Mother and the two of them gave me an invective-filled lecture on manners in stereo. Daddy was in charge of the invectives and Mother was in charge of looking heartbroken by my hunger-induced lapse of manners. Supper was over for me. I was told I could come out of the bedroom when I knew how to act and was ready to apologize to cousin Lawrence. I was so ashamed and mortified, I thought about running away from home, but I remembered Mother had made a lemon pie. I liked lemon pie better than I liked mashed potatoes, so I "sucked it up" and re-entered the family scene, apologized to cousin Lawrence, and waited for the pie to be doled out. From that moment on, I liked cousin Lawrence and mashed potatoes a little less than I had when the evening started. That night, I learned two things. First of all, I learned Mother and Daddy were deadly serious about those lessons in good manners they gave to us boys, and, secondly, I learned to avoid sitting at the end of the pass-line at suppertime.

As I think about the manners and behavioral norms expected of those of us growing up in the 1950s and 60s, I can't help but to compare them with what I observe to be acceptable today. In fairness, I guess one growing up in the

1920s probably saw changes in the manners and customs practiced by my generation. I really only feel qualified to compare our manners with those exhibited by today's kids. Whether you end up agreeing with my observations or not, at my age, I am more or less obliged to make them. It's what people my age do.

An absolute, carved-in-stone, etched-in-gold rule in the '50s was that adults were to be addressed using the honorifics of "ma'am" and "sir"—at least in Marshall. It was the golden rule of respecting one's elders. "No ma'am" and "yes sir" were essentials in showing you had been raised right. To fail to do so was an embarrassment to not only you, but also to your entire family. Being polite and respectful got a lot of corporal punishments reduced in severity.

When we raised our two children in the 1970s, we, along with other parents in the South and Southwest taught our kids to show elder-respect by using the ma'ams and sirs. This practice worked wonderfully until we moved to New England. When our daughter Mary Allison and our son Paul Scott came home from their first day in their new elementary school in Barrington, Rhode Island, they each brought home a note that instructed my wife and me to tell our children to stop using "ma'am" and "sir" when speaking with their teachers. They also advised us that neither child would be called by their first and middle names, just their first names. Per their new school administration, those were antiquated Southern practices that labeled our children as "misfits" among their new peers. Not wanting to brand our children as backwoods misfits, we played their game. I had just been given my first lesson in the "new" rules of manners and customs, much to my dismay. It was the first time we had lived north of the Mason-Dixon Line, and the dawning of our realization that "good manners" meant different things in the North than it did in the South. There were great, polite kids in the North, just as there were in the South. Manners were just different, and it took us a fair amount of time to adjust to the new customs. I'm not sure which version of manners was the best, but here's something to think about: you've often heard the term "Southern gentleman," right? Well, have you ever heard the term, "Northern gentleman"? I didn't think so. Again, the kids in the North were as nice as the kids in the South, it was just measured differently.

Growing up, I didn't like all of the grown-ups I knew. Some were real turds, some were selfish bullies, and some wouldn't pee on you if you were on fire. I did, however, have to show respect to all adults. The sir and ma'am monikers were granted to ALL adults, even the ones who didn't deserve it. That was okay with me because I respected and liked most of the adults in my life. In most all cases, my respect for them was returned tenfold in the kindness they showed me. In addition to respecting our elders, we also feared our elders. We knew they had more power than we did in a disagreement, and that if our spat went to our parents for arbitration, they would likely side with the adult. They had the power. Today, it seems to me that, too often, the kids have the power over the adults. Things change so fast in today's world, the value of an older person's wisdom is diminished, and, unfortunately, often lost. Too bad.

I wasn't allowed to sass my parents. It was non-negotiable; no sassing. Every kid I grew up with did some sassing, but there was a price to pay. In school, if we sassed a teacher, we got a spanking from either the teacher or the principal. If we ran home and told our parents, we usually got another spanking for having earned the one we got at school. Make no mistake about it, we were loved. We were cuddled, not coddled. If—make that when—I sassed at home, I was punished. It was considered disrespectful to parents to lay some "smart" talk on them. Is sass more prevalent today than it was in the 1950s and 1960s? I kind of think so. Don't you?

I am not saying all the kids today are rude or disrespectful. Old good manner stand-bys like "please" and "thank you" are still fashionable and show good breeding. A lot of kids today hold the door open for my wife and me. I guess the boys still hold it open for the girls. They do, don't they? We were taught to give our seat to women if there were no other seats available. Surely, parents still teach their kids to do the same today.

I cannot tell you how many times I was walking down the sidewalk with Mother when she took my elbow and put me between her and the street. That's one well-mannered practice I still have trouble remembering to do. When I forget to stand or walk between my wife and the street, I can still feel the wrath of Mother from on high. She was a stickler for that one! By the way, that custom began in the pre-sewer days when people who lived above their shops in the old downtowns would dump their slop jars from their second story windows onto the streets below. A gentleman always shielded his fair lady from the splashing sewage by standing or walking between it and his lady. That custom got a shot in the arm when wagons and cars would ride down the streets before paving became commonplace and splash mud up on the sidewalk. Being a gentleman in those days was a dirty job. I guess Mother, in another life, had been soiled by an errant turd or mud from a passing buggy, because she would nearly yank my arm out of place putting me between her and the street.

I guess manners that are important one day can become obsolete the next. Maybe since we have indoor toilets and sewers, and since our streets are now paved, standing between the street and a woman may be passé. Perhaps holding the door open for a woman or giving her your seat on a crowded bus is now an insult to women in search of equality. If so, I have insulted a whole lot of upwardly mobile women by showing them Old World courtesy. Sorry.

On another topic, when did it become okay to wear your hat indoors? We were taught a gentleman always took his hat or cap off before entering a building. I'm not sure why it was considered bad manners to wear your Stetson or baseball cap indoors, but it definitely was. Also, to me, it seemed stupid to wear a hat inside as it was not likely to rain in the living room and the overhead lights were never so bright you needed your hat brim to shade your eyes. Nowadays, men in restaurants eat with their hats on and "cool" guys under fifty often keep their caps on, usually backward. Who were the first mothers to tell their kids it was okay to wear their hats inside? What happened first? Did it become okay to wear hats indoors first, or did homes, public buildings and cafes stop making hat racks available first? Like I said, things change. I've never understood why country music singers wear their hats when performing indoors. If my mother had raised them, they wouldn't.

Showing courtesy to the opposite sex got me in trouble one time. It happened one afternoon when Daddy and I were riding through East Texas and decided to stop in Hughes Springs and say hello to our kin folks who lived there. While Daddy was in the house visiting with Aunt Maudie and Uncle Frank, I was in the backyard visiting with my cousins Mary Ellen and Sandy. Mary Ellen and I were both twelve at the time and had always been close. She was the closest thing I had to a sister. As we were catching up on stuff, a neighborhood boy named Ernie joined us. Everything was going just fine until Ernie announced that Mary Ellen was wearing a bra. I instantly took umbrage at his pronouncement, thinking that, in some way I couldn't quite get a handle on, he had insulted my cousin. In an ill-advised moment of chivalry, I jumped up from the swing I was sitting in and hollered, "She does not!" Ernie repeated his assertion, so I shoved him. He then shoved me back, so I slugged him. The fight was on, and, after we had exchanged quite a few blows, I reluctantly concluded that perhaps I had made a mistake in challenging his statement so vigorously. Ernie was one tough rascal. During the fisticuffs, I glimpsed my dad standing on the back porch drinking a cup of coffee and watching the two-boy melee. I quickly assumed Daddy would break up the fight and give his son some badly needed relief. Nope; that just wasn't the way Daddy did things. The fight continued, and, by this time, Ernie was well on the way to a convincing victory. Finally, Mary Ellen and Sandy both started wailing and trying to get in between Ernie and me. It worked. Ernie, fearing he would get in trouble, took off for home. Whew! My effort to do the well-mannered thing and defend my cousin's honor caused me to take a butt whippin'. By the way, Mary Ellen later whispered to me that she did, indeed, wear a bra.

Many of the manners we learned revolved around food and the act of eating it. My mother worked hours teaching me how to hold my knife, fork and spoon when eating. It wasn't a natural process, and, frankly, made little sense to me. At that point in my life, when it came to eating, I was much more focused on making certain I got my share of the food before my older brothers laid claim to it than I was on how to hold my utensils. Next to tying my shoes and telling time, knowing how to hold my fork, knife and spoon was about the hardest thing I had to learn. I eventually got it down, and, at long last, my mother could go to bed at night without worrying about me going "caveman" at some friend's dinner table. Part of proper eating etiquette involved learning to never put your elbows on the table and chewing with your mouth closed. One was taught to never talk with food in one's mouth, or, heaven forbid, "smack" their food. As I watch young people eating today, I see lots and lots of kids who were never taught these rules of etiquette. They often hold their utensils as though they are about to go to war, not enjoy a civil meal. Chewing and smacking are an all-too-common sight for this Texan boy.

I remember one day when I was in the sixth grade, I was getting ready to go to a pool party at Lynn Abney's house. My oldest brother, Homer, sat me down and reminded me of the "good manners" lessons Mother had always given us. In coaching me, he said the Abneys were likely to have a bowl full of potato chips and he instructed me on how to eat them. He told me it wasn't polite to grab a handful of chips, cram them into your mouth and crunch away. He said for me to take one at a time, place it between my lips, break it off with my lips and chew it quietly with my mouth closed. As he demonstrated this procedure, I had to admit it was a very quiet process. I practiced his system a couple of times, and he patted me on the back and pronounced me fit to eat chips at the Abney's. After wearing ourselves out in the pool, we all adjourned to the refreshments table on the patio. Sure enough, they had chips among a bunch of other snacks. I wanted to join right in with the assault on the snacks, but, remembering Homer's instructions, I approached the chips with a reverence they had seldom received. I calmly ate five or six chips the way he had told me to, but it felt more like I was conducting a religious rite than enjoying food at a rowdy pool party. I not only slipped from my pedestal of good manners, I leapt from it and joined all the other ravenous kids at the feeding trough. Despite my lapse in manners that day with the Abney's chips, I still practice brother Homer's chip-eating technique when in more formal environs. After all, if one of my heroes told me that was the way to eat chips, well, it must have been true.

Demonstrating good manners in public always made your parents and older relatives proud. Doing so showed the world you had been raised "right" and that your parents had earned the "Good Housekeeping Seal of Approval" when it came to child-rearing. I guess we were raised in a more disciplined environment than the generations that have followed. Right or wrong, it feels like later generations have stretched tolerance to an almost intolerable degree. The word "permissive" comes to mind when I think about the constricts in which kids function today. Today, rules seem to have fuzzy edges. We stopped at stop signs. The only time folks stop at stop signs today is if they must to avoid a cop or a collision. The term "rolling stop" is new to our language. When a stop light turned yellow, it used to mean start your stop. Today, it means gun it and haul ass. In fact, if you stop at a yellow light today, you will probably get rammed from behind or, at the very least, get a mean look, a honk and the finger from the irate guy behind you. The motto of today seems to be, "If you don't get caught, it ain't cheating." Even our government seems to have a "let it slide" attitude regarding certain laws. For example, we have laws concerning legal immigration, yet, we don't put much effort into enforcing them. Following rules appears to be an option these days, not a command.

In writing this chapter about manners, I've struggled with how to deal with farting. For some reason, farts have always been funny. We had a disaster drill when I was in junior high that required us to quietly proceed to the hallway, kneel and fold our arms around our head. While we were in that weird position, laughter began to ripple through the kneeling line. The tittering set off our science teacher, Mr. Bacher, and he traced its source to one giggling boy. Mr. Bacher confronted the boy and asked him what was so funny. The young man replied, "Scooter pooted." Mr. Bacher, who was a strict disciplinarian and believer in corporal punishment, moved to where Scooter was kneeling, put his foot on his back, and rammed him head-first into the locker next to which Scooter knelt. The giggling stopped. Did Scooter's poot mean he was ill-mannered, or just that he had gas? Like I said, I'm not sure how to handle farts in this discussion.

If the views I've expressed in this chapter on manners and customs offend you, so be it. Why should you be the only one walking around today feeling unoffended? Being offended by some thing or things seems to be quite popular. Clearly, we weren't as concerned with political correctness in the 1950s as we are today. I think it was more honest back then, but you are free to disagree. I suspect if we all had better manners today and followed the rules, far fewer of us would walk around in a state of being offended.

Chapter 21
And on to Junior High

The last day of school in 1958 was a big day for my classmates and me. Elementary school was over, and we were about to make the awesome transition into junior high. We had come this far together, and we would take this next step together, too. We couldn't wait to greet our new lives and move into a different arena for our adventures. We saw this move as a giant step into maturity. Little did we know just what a big step it would turn out to be.

It brought plenty of unexpected challenges to us Southsiders. Things like pimples, crackly voices and witnessing "booblets" pop out on the girls we had grown up with rattled our confidence. It seemed as though something big was hovering on our doorstep just waiting to walk in and change us profoundly. Our late-night thoughts turned to figuring out how to mesh with a large crop of unfamiliar kids from Marshall's other elementary schools and where we would fit in the new power structure that would evolve in this new setting. Unusual stuff began crowding our minds and nudging us out of our comfort zones.

Yep, the summer before our seventh grade brought about many changes, some obvious, some subtle. In my case, I graduated from Little League into the Babe Ruth League, from rubber cleats to metal cleats. Transitioning from the small Little League field to the full-sized baseball field was a giant leap. Playing ball against fifteen year olds, some of whom shaved, was a shock. It was hard going from being the star to sitting on the end of the bench.

It seemed to be the time when we put away childish games and began to focus on trying to be cool. We quit running footraces, and girls quit running at all. Torn jeans, dirty shirts or worn-out sneakers were "out." Clean and neat were "in." The Kiddie Show was now for "little kids." I occasionally pilfered splashes of my older brothers' cologne, and my best friend Terry bought a bottle of Jade East cologne. He used so much of it I could smell it from my front yard. I spent more time looking in the mirror, hoping to find a handsome, suave guy looking back at me. I began to learn how to handle disappointment.

I couldn't put my finger on exactly what was happening to me, but I knew I was going through some kind of rite of passage. The same was happening to Terry, Charlie, Tuck, Frank, Wist and the rest of our friends. When we got together, we just mostly talked and listened to records. More often than not, our talk was about girls, not Mickey Mantle's batting average or the styling breakthrough of the '57 Chevrolet. If we played, it was sports, not cops and robbers. Our giggles turned to laughter, and, as I noted earlier, the girls began to change, too. They acted differently and, yes, they didn't look the same, either. The entire summer seemed as if we were all being prepped for something new and different. That "new and different" turned out to be Marshall Junior High School and having our brains stolen and fried by something that took over our bodies, something that changed the direction of our lives—something called puberty. Well, that's another story. Stay tuned.

 # Acknowledgements

In writing *Mad Dogs, Marbles, and Rock Fights, A Memoir,* I prevailed on a group of special friends to read and evaluate many of the chapters before publication. I also asked them to validate the accuracy of my memories. They took their tasks to heart and reminded me of stories I had forgotten, corrected me when I was off-base and edited out lots of author-induced goofs. However, their greatest contribution to me was the cheerful encouragement they offered. That glorious group of friends included Kim Matthews, Dick and Bebe Cole, Karn Reinke, David Wist, Julee and Steve Hutchison, Terry and Jackie Weeks, Bob Power, and Sally Van Wert. Thanks, friends. I love you one and all.

Lastly, I tip my hat to my wife, Kay, my daughter Mary, and my son, Paul, for their editorial help. They helped me tremendously, while treating my fragile ego with kid gloves as they critiqued and improved my effort.

Made in the USA
Las Vegas, NV
21 June 2023

73711902R00154